THOUGHTS ON

THOUGHTS ON

LIFE LESSONS OF A VOLUNTEER FIREFIGHTER

Dr. Frank McCluskey

Professor of Philosophy,
Mercy College and Member,
Mahopac Falls Volunteer Fire Department

Writers Advantage
New York   Lincoln   Shanghai

Thoughts on Fire
Life Lessons of a Volunteer Firefighter

Writers Advantage
an imprint of iUniverse, Inc.

For information address:
iUniverse
2021 Pine Lake Road, Suite 100
Lincoln, NE 68512
www.iuniverse.com

ISBN: 0-595-22522-5

Printed in the United States of America

*This book is dedicated to firefighters
and emergency medical services workers everywhere.*

*They would give up their lives
to save someone they have never even met.*

Contents

And now here is my secret, a very simple secret; it is only with the heart that one can see rightly, what is essential is invisible to the eye.

Antoine de Saint-Exupery

Preface

Great is truth, fire cannot burn it, and water cannot drown it.

Alexander Dumas

Poetry comes nearer to vital truth than history.

Plato

We all live many lives. Sometimes we are brave and other times we are unsure of our steps. Often we know the way and other times we feel lost. There are times of initiation and times of mastery. There are periods we are proud and times we feel humble.

This is a book about two passions. It is a book about two lives lived side by side. In one of my lives I am a professor of philosophy. In that life, I love to make people think. I get excited when people ask questions about ideas they have believed for years. It has been my pleasure to hear, on occasion, that I have changed the way someone thinks. I enjoy being a guide in the exploration of that undiscovered country called "philosophy."

In my other life, I am a volunteer firefighter. In that world, I have broken down doors, smashed through the windows of cars, and stood inside fires that have melted the plumbing. In that life I have seen a baby being born. I have been present at the moment of death. There have been times when I have taken off my fire helmet, sat down, and cried because my heart was broken.

Volunteer firefighters often don't have the same time to think about ideas the way philosophy professors do. Firefighters live in a world where decisions must be made rapidly. They must always be prepared for that moment when life hangs in the balance. Firefighting can be a constant meditation on excellence, courage, and what it means to be human.

This book is a record of the intersection of these two passions. Each chapter begins by raising a philosophical question. We will look at ideas such as fear, happiness, and trust. Each chapter also contains a story from my experiences in the world of firefighting or emergency medical services. I have tried to weave together philosophical questions and stories of firefighting so that each one can illuminate the other.

The people depicted in this book are real people, the places depicted in this book are real places, and the events depicted in this book actually occurred. To make these stories easier to follow, I have combined incidents, characters, and times. Instead of recording the hundreds of characters and dozens of locations, I have compressed them into a book that is readable. In other words, I have taken real people, real events, and created a story. In the appendix I thank many of those whose stories have been included in this manuscript. The stories as they appear here are mostly true. You have my word on it. I have written an account of small-town life and the pleasures of everyday experience. I have tried to capture the rhythms of life of the small-town volunteer fire department. This is a book about the intersection of words and deeds. Most of all, this is the story of homecoming and forgiveness. It is an American tale.

Acknowledgements

More people have helped me than I can acknowledge here. I include only those few names that deserve special mention although a thousand names are in my heart and on the tip of my tongue. First of all I would like to thank my students who have truly taught a professor of philosophy the real meaning of wisdom. Thanks to Dr. Lucie Lapovsky, Dr. Carol Moore, Dr. Louise Feroe, Dr. Ann Grow, Dr. Francis Mahoney, and Professor Andy Joppa of Mercy College who give me the freedom to be myself. Dr. Jim Munz of Western Connecticut University has helped me with many of the ideas in this book. I also want to thank Ted McGrath for his constant friendship. Reverend Robert McCluskey, psychotherapist Lynn Berrett, Dr. Joshua Berrett, Laura McCluskey, and Joseph Macchiarulo helped refine the ideas of the text. Thanks to Pat Strusarre, Jack Casey, Dr. Boria Sax, and Dr. Howard Canaan for sympathetic readings of the original manuscript. Thanks to Fire Chief Jimmy Deigan and Chief Randy Tompkins. Many of the stories in these pages are paraphrases of stories I heard from them. Thanks to Dean Rosemary Murray, Denis Arvay of IBM, Dr. Joel Feimer, Dr. Robert Schachat, and Ryk Greco for their encouragement in this project. I would like to thank my long-distance philosophical friends, Dr. George Teschner of the Philosophy Department of Christopher Newport College, and Dr. Bill Maker, Chairman of the Philosophy Department of Clemson University. Thanks to Shiela, Brandon, and Kelly for their support at the beginning and end of this project. Special thanks to Marguerite for her endless patience with this manuscript.

1

Teaching, or lessons from snowflakes and fire

Oh for a muse of fire, that would alight the brightest heaven of invention.

Shakespeare

Take my hand. Take my hand and let us, together, stand inside the fire. Once inside the fire, with its angry reds, dancing oranges and tongues of scarlet, some part of us will no doubt feel afraid. As the black smoke curls around us like a python and begins to steal our light, we will be afraid of burning or choking in the hot darkness. But if we can get past that fear, if we can stand still and pay attention to our feelings, there are lessons to be learned here, inside the furnace. These lessons will reveal who we are and what is in our hearts. They are lessons about contentment, fear, trust and happiness. These are the answers to the questions that the great philosophers have asked since time began. As a professor of philosophy, I was just a little surprised to find out that the answers could be found inside of a burning building.

If you met me on the tree-lined path between classes, you would probably guess that I am a college professor. I'm in my forties and my black hair is almost all gone. I wear glasses and I'm usually weighted down with books and papers. At school I like to wear striped ties and herringbone jackets. I often walk with my students or other professors and talk about ancient books or poetry.

For many years, when I saw the world through the eyes of a professor of philosophy, I wrote in my journal about books I had read: Greek dramas, the writings of Chinese mystics, or French novels. As a college teacher, I'm expected to write and reflect on such ideas.

When I became a member of a volunteer fire department, more and more of my reflections centered on fire and the lessons I was learning in the world of the firefighter. In my journal, page by page, images of Proust and Plato gave way to thoughts on the power of and fascination with fire. I began to see the world in a new way. I began to value simple experiences and pleasures that I had almost forgotten. I sailed away from the port of books and libraries and into the rough seas of action and commitment, with fire as the beacon lighting the way.

When people find out that a philosophy professor is a volunteer firefighter, they are often surprised. Talking about philosophy and acting without hesitation at a fire or ambulance call seem to be totally different activities and to require different approaches to life. It's difficult for people to imagine the same person doing both.

Professing philosophy and fighting fires are not as different as you might think. Both pursuits can be looked upon as roads that can lead us to the mirror in which we must all one day look. They can lead us to the moment of truth, the moment when we understand something mysterious and profound about life. Truth can be found in ancient texts, but it also waits for us deep inside a burning house. For there, with the roof caving in and the floor on fire, a person can learn secrets about himself that can't be found in the reading room of a college library.

Philosophizing and firefighting have many traits in common. They both require that you constantly think and question. They both ask that you carefully review all details until you are sure nothing has been missed. They both insist that you never assume anything.

I've come to realize that in many ways, fire and we humans are alike. Unlike the other three elements of the universe imagined by the ancient Greeks—earth, water, and air—fire is always changing and transforming. It's different from more stable entities like earth, lakes, or rocks. Fire is born where it didn't exist before. It breathes. It eats. It grows. Eventually, like us, it dies.

Fire investigators talk of the "path" of a fire as if it has its own purpose and direction. It follows its own path, seeking nourishment. It grows and searches, aspiring upwards. Like us, it comes into this world for a flickering instant, always changing, at each moment different and new.

Poets and philosophers have thought that our souls are like flames when we believe, love, or aspire. Shakespeare called for "a muse of fire" to inspire him, and Robert Frost rhymed it with the word "desire." When our own fire goes out and we leave this world, it is customary in many places to remember the departed soul by lighting a candle.

As a firefighter, I try to extinguish fires as quickly as possible. But in the classroom, I spend my time trying to light young minds on fire and then feeding that flame. When philosophy makes us awake and alive, the warmth is wonderful. The light of reason makes us think about our lives, what is good and noble, and where we should seek for truth.

When we begin an Introduction to Philosophy class at the college, I like to show students the difference between what we think we know and what is real. We begin with a simple question to which most people think they know the answer. I ask them, "Are any two snowflakes alike?" They almost always give the same answer, "No two snowflakes are alike." Then I ask them another question. "How do you know that that's true?" Now the class is getting interesting. We begin to think; we begin to wake up and really look at the question. After a while, we agree that we are not sure if two snowflakes could be exactly alike. Then I pose one more question. "Could anybody know that this statement is true?" Of the billions and billions of snowflakes that fall in a single storm, who can say whether two identical snowflakes can fall or not? We understand that what we thought was true may not be so. But this lesson is not about snowflakes. It is not about anything small or unimportant. It illustrates the most profound truth we could ever grasp. We have learned not to assume. The snowflakes have been our teachers.

Fire, like snowflakes, can teach us, but it is an unforgiving teacher. The lessons it teaches have to be studied well, for the consequences can be severe if they are not heeded.

When fighting a fire, a firefighter cannot assume that all of the residents are safely out of the house. Firefighters cannot assume that a floor on fire will still be intact when they turn to escape to the cool of the outside. When they pull a flashlight off the fire truck, they cannot assume it will work. It must be checked before it goes inside the fire. As in the world of philosophy, in the world of the firefighter, where television sets melt and roofs collapse, assuming will not do.

I came to the world of fire after having spent my life searching for meaning in books and words because I still felt that something was missing. When people feel that way, they sometimes do crazy things. Some people buy sports cars, some people learn to sky dive, but I chose to do something far more dangerous. I joined our local volunteer fire department and walked into a world of large red trucks surrounded by chrome and leather helmets that smelled of smoke. I had entered the world of fire and those who understand it. I had spent my time teaching others about snowflakes and now I was to become a student of fire.

One of the concepts I had learned in college was that you have to be open and humble if you're going to learn anything. Here is a Zen story that will explain this. "A famous professor of philosophy, who was very arrogant and full of himself went to visit a Zen Master in Kyoto. The professor sat down and the Master offered him a cup of tea. The professor accepted and held out his cup as the Master poured. The Master filled the cup to the rim and then it began to overflow. The professor shouted that the cup was full. The Master smiled. 'You come to me like this cup, full of ideas and opinions. How can I teach you if you do not come here empty?'"

Remembering this story, I went to the fire department not as "Doctor" or "Professor" but as Frank, a thirty-five-year-old rookie who swept the floor, polished the trucks, and listened when the seasoned old smoke-eaters talked with reverence and humor about fire and what it could do. I did not tell them what my other job was. I wanted to be judged as a human being, not as a professor. When asked why I had so much free time, I explained it in a way that was partly true and easy to explain. I told them I did "shift work."

In time, I learned how to raise ladders, force open doors, and use an air bottle when the air was too hot to breathe. I learned how to stop a victim's bleeding and do CPR so that I could qualify to ride the two ambulances our department operated. But most of all, I watched and listened and eventually I began to learn about fire—but not from words. I tried to let the fire itself be my teacher. That's what firefighters do.

In the world of the firefighter, I found what had eluded me in the texts of Plato and Aristotle. There are many paths. Like fire, I too, followed a path. My path led me inside the fire. There, amidst the flames, I learned truths about myself that I had always wanted to know.

My evolution from a bookish college professor to one of the more active members in a busy volunteer fire department is a story that takes a little time to tell. I had to learn not just about hoses and axes but also how to approach life in a different manner. Somewhere on the way, along with fires, car wrecks, and chaos, I found my answers to the questions that philosophers have searched for since time began.

Buddhists say that when you are ready to learn, a teacher will appear. They also say, "Even a stone can be a teacher." Wherever we have come from and wherever we're going, I feel that we are here for some reason. We are here to learn. Some lessons are easy to learn. Others, ones we don't fully comprehend the first time, will be repeated until we get them right. If we are open and know how to listen, anything can be our teacher, even things as different as snowflakes and fire.

2

Setting the Stage, or how to be content wherever you are

A place belongs forever to whoever claims it hardest, remembers it most obsessively, wrenches it from itself, shapes it, renders it, loves it so radically that he remakes it in his own image.

Joan Didion

Every spring, when the apple blossoms are at their peak and the seas of daffodils are softly fading, thunderstorms roam the Hudson River Valley. Some storms drift north from the southerly parts of the ocean, which the Dutch, who first settled the place, used to call the "Zee." But mostly, the storms come down from the Catskill Mountains northwest of here, the same mountains that Washington Irving wrote about in his famous tale *Rip Van Winkle*.

The yellow daffodils wave as the storms bring their cool rains and warm breezes. These spring storms announce themselves long before they arrive. You can see flashes of fire on the horizon and hear the low moans and angry growls of the thunder. Like wrathful deities forever doomed to wander on the four winds, the storms drift up and down the valley, restlessly active, always in motion. Many people live their lives like those spring storms, producing a lot of noise and activity. They are so restless that they never remain in one spot for too long, never take time to focus on a single moment, and never really feel content. They are looking for what they always feel is just beyond their grasp. So they go on seeking, looking elsewhere for what they believe they cannot find in the life they are living. Philosophers and poets have known for centuries that contentment has nothing to do with places or possessions or money; rather, it is a state of mind. You can be content when you realize that wherever you are contains its own truth, its own rhythm, and its own wisdom. I remember someone once remarked to me that he didn't like daffodils because they "don't last for very long." Two hundred years ago, the poet William Wordsworth looked at those same daffodils and joyfully described them as "tossing their heads in sprightly dance." The poet, John Keats, was inspired to write, "A thing of beauty is a joy forever."

If contentment is a state of mind, one does not need to go to Tibet or Stonehenge to learn what is important in life. It can be learned anywhere. Any place can be your library, and its people, houses, streets, and fields can be your texts. Within those texts, to echo Keats again, "is all we know and all we need to know".

People spend their lives pursuing different goals. Some spend their time and energy looking for love, some search for pleasure, some security, some power, and others respect. But in the end, you might say that all of these pursuits are aiming at the same goal. Everyone wants to be content.

To illustrate what I mean by contentment, I will tell you about an unlikely place that makes many people content, a place that people aren't too quick to leave if they can help it—our fire district in Mahopac Falls, New York. Most of the firefighters have lived there all of their lives. They're slow to change and careful about new ideas. With the exception of burning buildings, the Mahopac Falls volunteer firefighters don't like to rush into things too quickly. Patience is something that the old-time firefighter had plenty of. I, myself, am usually a little short in this department. But I am going to ask for your patience over the next few pages. Before I can tell you stories of flaming explosions and moments of life and death, the stage must be set.

If you were driving on one of the local roads in the hilly region north of Westchester County, New York, you might pass the Mahopac Falls Volunteer Fire Department and never know it. It sits off the main road and looks like most of the other firehouses in America. It is a two-story brick building. There is a parking lot and a manicured lawn. In front the American flag flies and there is a picnic table off to the side. At the foot of the parking lot there is a little bridge and a stream that runs under it. The stream meanders into woods and disappears. It looked like an ordinary building the first time I saw it. It seemed that way to me the first time I saw it. I would have never guessed all of the amazing and heroic adventures connected with that building.

Although the hamlet of Mahopac Falls is just fifty miles north of New York City, it might as well be a thousand miles away. It belongs to that part of the country that hasn't changed much in the last hundred years. These are places in America today where the corner grocer still knows his customers by name and the local barber cuts the hair of little boys whose grandfathers once sat in that same old worn leather chair. It's a place where white steeples on the local churches still stand tall against the blue sky and the autumn maples are bright orange and red.

Not far from Mahopac Falls, twenty miles down the Hudson River, is the place where Washington Irving told us Rip Van Winkle found out the secret of thunder. Irving portrayed Rip as an old Dutchman who preferred not to face his responsibilities in life, spending his time instead hanging around the village, sipping beer, and talking with his lazy pals about the weather.

The story goes on to say that one day Rip wandered off into those mountains, looking, as many of us do, for that elusive something that we always think must be someplace else. Deep in those enchanted mountains, Rip met some mysterious strangers enjoying a game of bowling. The sounds of those magic bowling balls, we are told, created the sound of thunder that echoed in the Catskill Mountains and cascaded down the Hudson River Valley. Rip went to sleep there for twenty years and woke up to find that much had changed.

I think that if Rip had slept for 250 years instead of just twenty, he might have found out that although some things had changed, other things around here are still the same. Many people here, some of Dutch descent, still avoid hard work and talk about how life was better in the "old days." Like Rip and his pals, many of them are just trying to make it through the day. Many dreamers still avoid cleaning the gutters by escaping from the house for a few hours. Some even hide out at the fire department.

Mahopac Falls, tucked away in the mountains, has no major roads running through it. It is still woodsy enough for an occasional pheasant and fox to wander into your backyard. There are so many deer that I almost hit two last year driving the Falls' ambulance.

There is a little store that's the spiritual center of the Falls. It is the Red Mills Market, owned by the Jedleka family, It has a long history in our part of the world. If you want to know what's happening in town, Ron Jedleka in Red Mills will know. There is talk about the weather, whose road is going to be repaved first, and whose little league team is doing well. National events aren't too much on the minds of these people most of the time. This is a neighborhood store with a local focus. In the same little row of stores there is a barbershop, a dry cleaners, a liquor store and the pub, where the firefighters stop on occasion to compare notes and have a game of darts.

A couple of old clapboard churches populate the Falls. Right across the street from the fire department is the old Mahopac Falls Baptist Church, built in 1832 and remodeled in 1868. Sometimes the firefighters open the doors to the engine room on a nice day, sit in old folding wooden chairs and watch the clouds roll by the steeple. The steeple has not been straight for more than fifty years. There is some debate about which way the church steeple is leaning. Some of the old-timers say it leans to the left and some say it leans to the right. The first time I heard this conversation, I thought we should get a frame and a plane and solve the riddle once and for all. But after a while, I realized that would take all of the fun out of a fifty-year-old debate. On a hot morning in summer we will tune the radio to our local radio station, WHUD, and listen to the morning DJs Mike and Casey playing Sly and Family Stone's *Hot Fun in the Summertime*. We sit and listen and watch the clouds roll by.

Big ash and maple trees line the Falls' main street, which is called simply, "6N." A few of the oldest trees stand right in front of the Baptist Church. In summer they provide cooling shade and in autumn their colors are spectacular. There is a small cemetery behind the church. Some of the old firefighters are buried there, on a hillside that slopes down towards the brook. If you were to take a stroll through the cemetery, you would find the names of some of the old families in town: the Agors, the Austins, the

Tompkins and the Smiths. It's a simple little grassy area with nothing too fancy. The markers are mostly plain granite stones.

There are three schools in the Falls, and protecting them keeps the firefighters on their toes. There are also several nursery schools. Up on 6N is Noah's Ark where Ms. Pat guides the lives of dozens of toddlers and preschoolers. There are two schools on Myrtle Avenue. Myrtle Avenue is where Myrtle Brady lived most of her life. She's the deceased wife of our oldest active member, Art Brady who, at eighty, occasionally still comes along on a fire or ambulance call just to watch. Art is short, bald, thin, and athletic looking. He likes to have a beer once in a while, does a lot of fundraising for local charities and still does a mean cha-cha at firehouse dances.

Mahopac Falls is hilly and has many lakes and ponds. The location of these ponds is important to the firefighters because there are only a few hydrants in the entire hamlet and these don't always work. To get water, which is the lifeblood of firefighting, the firefighters back the trucks up to the ponds, drop in a suction hose with a strainer, and start suctioning up the water. The firefighters call this "drafting." They draft from ponds, streams, swamps, and from the big lakes. They have even been known to "borrow" the water in somebody's in-ground swimming pool to put out a fire in a neighbor's house.

Some people ask what firefighters do for water when the temperature gets below freezing and ice covers all of the water sources in town. It's simple. They take axes and saws out onto the ice, sometimes in the dark of night, to cut a hole big and deep enough to get water. If one of the firefighters has been ice fishing nearby, he finds the spot and drops in a suction hose.

The Falls even has a little airport that isn't much more than a grassy field for single-engine planes. On most days in spring, summer, and fall, you can see them taking off low over the firehouse, banking past the steeple of the Baptist church, and climbing into the clouds. The drone of the little engines can be heard over the fire house as we sit on our chairs in front of the open firehouse doors and watch.

Most of the big old barns have long since burned down. Those ancient hay barns were just fires waiting to happen, and once they got going, they burned hot and fast. There used to be a chicken farm up by Friendly Road until a fire broke out in one of the hen houses. The whole coop was burning when the fire department arrived. By the time they started the interior attack, most of the chickens were already cooked. Twelve thousand chickens died in that fire. You can guess the stories that have been told over the years about what was served for dinner that night down at the firehouse. I am never quite sure if the old-timers are serious about that story or pulling my leg.

The whole town is wrapped around Lake Mahopac, the big lake that gives our town its name. The road around it is over six miles long. The life and seasons of the town revolve around the lake. In the old days, the town used to be a big resort area for vacationers from New York City. There were six big hotels on Lake Mahopac. Some of them had over two hundred rooms. They had huge porches with large pillars facing the lake. Dozens of rocking chairs were lined up in summer. There was bathing and boating every day of the summer. At night, the visitors would dress for dinner, men in striped jackets and straw hats, the women in elaborate dresses. After dinner, there was dancing to the music of live bands on the big ballroom floors. Some of the old firefighters were just children when the last of the hotels were still in business. They used to row out in boats on the darkened lake under the stars. There, they would listen to the music from the hotel ballrooms come wafting over the water. The railroad used to stop nearby; a horse and carriage would bring the guests the rest of the way. Two of the hotels had carriages drawn by four horses each. One team was jet black and the other was snowy white. The two carriages would sometimes race through town on their way to the big hotels.

All of the hotels had their own gardens and tennis courts. There was even a steamboat with a brass band that would take people dancing in the moonlight on Lake Mahopac. Fire consumed most of the big hotels years ago. They smoldered for days when they burned down. The historical society in the center of town displays old pictures, now brown with age, showing men in derbies and women in bustled dresses with parasols walking through gardens by the shore as sails dotted the lake on a summer's afternoon. Around the turn of the century, there was even a popular song about Lake Mahopac.

The railroad, the hotels, and the steamboat are all gone now. Sometimes when I look out over the lake, I can imagine the music, the gaiety, and the bustle.

A great deal about the fire department has changed. Today we have two stations. The main station has offices, a meeting hall, and a bar on the second story. The engines, trucks, and ambulances are on the first floor. If you were to walk in the meeting hall, you would find it lined with pictures of ex-chiefs, big fires, and heroic deeds. Many things, however, have not changed. Some of the retired firefighters spend their time at the firehouse puttering around, just the way they used to do fifty years ago. The firehouse is a simple place with simple beginning. When the fire department was founded in 1937, a few men sat in the back of the Agor Brothers' grocery store and wrote the charter on the back of a piece of butcher paper.

Maybe, like Rip Van Winkle, they like to get out of the boredom of everyday life and have someplace else to go. For Rip, it was the tavern; for the firefighters, it's the firehouse. There's a horseshoe pit behind the building where some of the old-timers "throw a pretty good shoe." During the summer, Charlie Locke plays often with Art Brady. Charlie has been in the fire department for twenty-four years and Art has been in for fifty. Charlie is trim and usually sports a tan. He always has a joke to tell or a story to relate. He is one of the regular "senior citizens" who can often be found at the firehouse keeping an eye on things. Both Art Brady and Charlie Locke are retired and have plenty of time to sharpen their game while telling stories of the great fires of old. They have played thousands of games of horseshoes with each other over the years and it is still a stiff competition. You can hear them arguing about whose shoes are closest to the stake. If you talk to them alone, you will find that each one thinks that the other one isn't quite as good. You know when summer has come when you hear Charlie say, "Hey man, how about some shoes?" We get the rake and the horseshoes and walk up the hill. We stand in the summer sun and pitch those shoes waiting for Artie or Charlie to yell "Ringer!"

Yes, if Rip Van Winkle walked out of the woods and found himself standing in front of the Mahopac Falls Volunteer Fire Department today, he would probably feel right at home. He might have a game of shoes with Art and Charlie or maybe he would sit and chat with Walt Swarm, who grew up many years ago on a nearby farm milking cows and herding cattle. Although Walt is Swedish, his white hair and sparkling blue eyes make him look a lot like the Dutch who originally settled here three hundred years ago. He is short and muscular, forever chewing on a cigar. He was chief back in '54, knows every road and family in the Falls and he still drives the trucks for a working fire. Walt is a no-nonsense old-timer who gives us heck if something about the trucks isn't just the way it should be. I sometimes wonder if Walt isn't the reincarnation of firefighters in this town from an earlier time, a kind of guardian angel. He is forever working on the trucks and spends a good deal of time complaining that the world was a better place in the "old days."

Walt is as gruff and rough a trucker as you have ever met, but for some reason he took me under his wing and began to teach me about trucks, water, and fire. It was from him, more than anyone, that I learned the art of emergency work. For the first two years in the fire department he called me "you." I knew him for years before he found out I was a college professor. When he finally realized it he was surprised.

"A pa'fessor! Are you kiddin'?" Now he calls me "Doc" when I get everything exactly right, which is rarely, and "pa'fessor" when he's pointing out some spot I missed on the truck or something I did wrong at an ambulance call.

When I first arrived at the firehouse, I had all sorts of ideas about how to make things "better" at the Falls. It took a while for Walt and the old-timers to slow me down, but they took the time. Time passes at a leisurely pace at the firehouse. The firefighters sit and listen for the spring storms or watch the old-timers toss horseshoes as they talk about people they have known for fifty years.

If I close my eyes, I can imagine Rip Van Winkle at the Falls firehouse. I think he might enjoy a good cigar with Walt. Or the two of them might take a short walk to the pub and have a cold beer on a hot day. Maybe old Rip would be content to sit on a chair in front of the engine room with the big bay doors open and the engines shining. Listening for spring storms wandering far away, he would smile his sleepy smile. He could sit with us and watch the clouds roll by the steeple of the Baptist Church and add his two cents worth to the ongoing discussion about whether it leans to the left or the right.

3

Arrival, or how to renew your life

To travel is often more pleasurable than to arrive.

Author Unknown

There are moments in life after which we know we will never be the same. Life may go on for a long time without a major incident. Suddenly, something changes in a way that we perhaps did not even think possible. These are moments we all remember: the night we graduated from high school, the night a loved one died, or the day we met someone we love. We recall births, weddings, the last day we left one world, or the day we arrived in another.

The French philosopher, Jean-Paul Sartre, focused on those moments. It was his view that certain moments reveal our true character and scream out what we only whisper in our hearts. All of Sartre's writings reveal the search for arrivals and departures, those defining moments that make each of us who we are.

I'll never forget my arrival at the Falls firehouse. A few weeks after I applied, I got a phone call from a gruff old smoke-eater who told me to come down to the firehouse to get sworn in at the department's monthly meeting. I didn't know what to expect and I almost didn't go to that first meeting. It was, by the way, the second time I had applied. I had filled out an application about ten years earlier and had never heard from the fire department. I assumed that I had been rejected. It turns out they lost my application. Although firefighters and Emergency Medical Services (EMS) workers are selfless and giving, they are sometimes remiss in doing paperwork. Years later one of the "boys" thought he remembered using the application to wipe the oil off a dipstick on one of the engines. If you believe, as I do, that the universe has its own sense of timing, you trust that every moment has its own special quality. Perhaps it hadn't been time ten years earlier for me to make that step. Perhaps other parts of my life had to be worked out before I was ready for the lessons of fire.

When I arrived at the firehouse to be sworn in, a tough-looking guy was standing at the front door. I nodded and smiled. He didn't smile back; he just turned around and walked inside. I gulped hard and followed. To avoid sticking out like a sore thumb, I wore my oldest sweatshirt, avoiding any logo that contained words like "Yale" or "Lux et Veritas." I was wearing my oldest pair of jeans and my worn-out sneakers. I looked as raw and rough as a middle-aged college professor can pretend to be. The meeting hall was packed with gruff-looking old men who had been fighting fires for fifty years. By profession, they were truckers, policemen, butchers, electricians, and paid firefighters from New York City who still found the energy to volunteer during their free shifts. Although the fire department had a handful of female members, none of them were at that meeting. There were guys wearing baseball caps that said "Mack Trucks." On the front on those hats was a picture of a bulldog standing on the word "Mack" looking as vicious as a pit bull with rabies. The "boys" were smoking cigars and cursing. These were not the type of people I was used to dealing with in faculty meetings. These were guys who knew about drive shafts, power saws, and hose pressure. I knew nothing about this equipment. I sat there in the back with my arms crossed and tried not to look too nervous. They started talking about the "pump capacity on a tanker." I had no idea what they were talking about. After the meeting was over they opened the bar in the next room and started talking about a big fire they'd had a few days before. I sat there alone, listening to tales of floors on fire below and flaming ceilings above. I was sitting among firefighters who had walked through that and lived.

I sat at the bar near Tommy Stasiak. He was in his late twenties, had a blond gunfighter moustache, and correction officer's vocabulary. He was careful to say "corrections officer" instead of "prison guard," I guess for the same reason that college professors hate to be called "teachers." Tommy had a rough and colorful way of speaking that always put things in a new perspective. I remember once having a conversation with him about local politics. He ended it by saying, "One hand washes the other and both hands wash the face." I am never sure what he means by sayings like that, but I love to listen to that man talk! But despite all of this colorful language, there is a calm and focus about him that makes him a good man to be near when a fire gets hot.

Tommy was sharing a beer, a cigar, and stories with the crusty old smoke-eater I'd seen at the door, Walt Swarm. Like the great Zen Masters of old, Walt tried to discourage and scare me for the first five years, just to see if I was a serious candidate. It is a kind of hazing or initiation that separates the wheat from the chaff. Walt loves to argue and he and Tommy were having a heated discussion about how they had attacked the fire.

Before I even sat down at the bar, I was told the rules about firehouse drinking. It seemed that years ago, you could have a couple of beers and fight fires. Today, the rules are different. At our firehouse, if you have one sip of one beer, you are out of service for three hours. That means no fire or ambulance calls. The firefighters usually arrange it so that some of them are on duty and some of them are off duty. This is a rule about which they are very strict. I found out, as a member of the firehouse, that if someone breaks this rule, our department deals with it quickly and harshly.

That first night, I sat on the chair and listened. The Mahopac Falls Volunteer Fire Department is a closed society. Many of the members in the firehouse had grown up there and they had been through a lot together. I was the new kid on the block. I wondered how I would ever have the time or the energy to win their acceptance. Although I had physically set foot in the firehouse, I hadn't really arrived yet as a member of the group. The radio was tuned to WHUD. The evening DJ, Andy Bale, was playing Randy and the Rainbows singing *Denise.* I finished up my beer and went downstairs to the engine room floor where the trucks stood silently in the dark. I walked alongside one of the big red engines and looked at all of the gauges, dials, and handles. Helmets were hanging over the railings with burn marks and scrapes all over them. Touching the fire gear and feeling their still-wet insides, I wondered how each of those burns and scrapes had been earned. I wondered what kinds of texts these helmets were and how one learned to read them. On the sides of the truck hung ladders and axes and other tools whose names only firefighters knew. The truck smelled of smoke. In time I would come to know that smell so well that if I was on a truck coming into a good working fire, I could gauge by that smell how tough a night it was going to be. It's a smell that gets into your pores and your hair.

Once you know it, it's a smell you will never forget. I looked at all of the hoses lying in complicated patterns on the back of the trucks and wondered what kind of world I had discovered so close to home. I was new to this world, a stranger in a strange land, and I wondered if I would last.

When you first join, the members assume you don't know anything about fighting fires. In my case, this was a valid assumption. Before being allowed to go into a real fire, you had to be in the department for a number of months and take several courses that taught you about fighting fires. In the department I joined, you had to take more than fifty hours of training before you could get close to a fire. I'm not saying that the membership didn't trust my knowledge of firefighting, but when the veterans showed me an axe, they taped a message to the pointed tip. It was meant as a joke but also to show me how little I knew about fire fighting. On the sharp tip on the head of the axe the sticker said simply, "Hold by other end."

When a fire department arrives at an emergency scene, there is no room for errors. A single mistake or miscalculation can result in injury or even death. To make sure this doesn't happen, firefighters spend a great deal of time practicing for the real fires.

A few weeks after I joined the fire department, I started my training. The firefighters loaned me a helmet, coat, and boots. They took me and a few other new recruits to the training center to show us the ropes and to teach us how to think like firefighters.

At the fire department, classes consist of two parts: lectures, and what the firehouse calls the "practical." I was really great at the lecture part. I read my book, studied all the terms, and always had my hand raised to answer every question in detail. But the "practical" part gave me some difficulty. People who can answer all the questions sometimes have a hard time doing practical things. Others who are good at doing things sometimes have a difficult time explaining themselves. This is where we get the ideas of "book smart" and "street smart."

I remember the first time our rookie class had to put up a ladder. When there is a fire, ladders have to go up quickly so that firefighters can get up on the roof in a hurry. The ladders we carry on our truck are thirty-five foot extension ladders. It takes four people to get one off the truck and set it up. After we get it off the truck, we stand it up, and then we have to pull a rope called a "fly" to raise it to its full extension. These ladders are long and heavy. Doing this right takes coordination and practice.

We dressed in our fire-fighting gear, pulled the ladder off the truck, staggering as we carried it. When we stood the ladder up, Tommy Stasiak, who was teaching the class, came over, cigar in mouth, and looked over everything very carefully. He congratulated us on an excellent job and told us we had made only one small mistake. We had placed the ladder upside down. He said this would "make it a little difficult to raise."

Walt Swarm was standing back by the truck laughing as we took the ladder down and switched it around. You have to hold the ladder by the sides or "rails" with the palms of your hands, while another person pulls the fly, raising the extension part of the ladder into the air. You cannot hold the ladder by the rungs because it might drop down and take off your fingers. You hold it by the rails and listen to it clank as it is extended and wobbles in the air. It took us forever to get it right. Eventually we raised it and leaned it against the tower, which was four stories tall. Stasiak came up to me, chomping on an unlit cigar. "Now climb it!"

I didn't want to let him know that I got nosebleeds standing on a chair to change a light bulb. Being a guy, I was more worried about appearing cowardly than about falling. I climbed up about ten feet and looked back. He was smiling. "Why'd ya stop? Keep goin'!"

I turned and climbed about four or five rungs from the top. I was now thirty feet over a concrete parking lot and there was a strong wind. The ladder was up against a window on the top of the building. I felt my hands sweating inside my gloves. I looked down. Tommy was still looking at me. "You're not at the top yet!"

I took a deep breath and climbed to the top, feeling the aluminum ladder wobble beneath me. My heart was pounding so hard that I thought it was going to explode! I thought I had made it now and looked below in triumph. But it wasn't over yet. I heard a familiar voice from thirty-five feet below. "What are you waiting for? Get into that window! There might be a child that needs to be rescued!"

Gingerly, I put my leg out into the air high above the parking lot and held my breath. I felt my foot rest on something inside the window. I took one trembling hand from the ladder and grabbed the inside of the window. I closed my eyes and let go of the ladder as I pulled myself inside the tower. For a moment, my body was riding on the wind between the ladder and the building. Suddenly I was inside. I had passed my first real test, but not with flying colors.

Fires in modern houses produce great quantities of toxic smoke. Burning televisions, VCRs, chairs, and other plastic materials produce smoke that can kill someone with a single breath. Firefighters wear masks attached to air bottles so they can function in this environment. This toxic smoke is heavy and dark. You can't see a thing inside a fire and you have to get used to feeling your way around. You must know where you are without using your eyes. You must know where you came in and how you can get out without using your eyes. Firefighters call this "seeing with your hands."

The Fire Training Center has a building called the "smokehouse." This is not a place where you make sausages. It is a concrete block building with no windows and only one door. It has walls, rooms, beds, and dummies inside. The drill is simple. You are supposed to go in with a partner, find any dummies, and bring them outside. This is called "search and rescue," and every fire department in America knows how to do this. They have to. If you think someone is trapped in a fire, you have to go inside and carry him or her out. Imagine being crammed in a hot space where you can't see. Imagine not knowing what kind of room you are in. This is not just a classroom exercise. If you are searching for someone and you do not find him quickly the consequences can be deadly.

To make the smokehouse seem like a real fire, trainers use a smoke machine to fill the closed building with smoke and make it impossible to see, just like in a real fire. This smoke is non-toxic but it does impair your vision. We put air bottles on our backs and wear air masks along with our helmets, boots, hats, and gloves. Inside the mask, the air flows only when you inhale, a very confining and scary feeling at first. You get down on all fours with your partner and crawl into the smokehouse. You have to crawl because heat rises, so the coolest place in a fire is closest to the ground. Feeling the air blowing on your face, you grab the coat of the other firefighter and plunge into the darkness.

Once you're inside, the door is closed behind you to keep the smoke in. It's interior walls are portable so that the inside configuration can be changed between crews to create more confusion. You stumble, you bump into walls, and sometimes, new members panic. The first time I went in, I felt as if I was going to suffocate in that tight mask compounded by the blackness of the smoke. I wanted to stand up, rip the mask off, and breathe deeply. I knew that this would be a mistake. I fought my fear and kept going until we found the dummy and dragged it back outside. I pulled off the mask and took a deep breath of fresh air. Stasiak took the cigar out of his mouth and yelled, "Next!" Even if you do a good job, fire-fighters are not very quick to congratulate you.

Eventually you get the hang of being inside a burning building where you can't see anything. You grope, fall, and slowly start to understand how it works. You never get comfortable inside a fire, but in time you learn what to expect.

The fire department in my town has an EMS section that runs the ambulance service for our fire district. There is a good deal of training that has to be done on the ambulance before a new member can go on any calls. There are four people on an ambulance crew. First, there is the driver. Next, there is an Emergency Medical Technician (EMT), or First Responder, who rides as crew chief and is responsible for patient care. The third person is an experienced hand that the crew chief can call upon to get information and treat the patient. The fourth person is someone who is there to observe and to learn. During the first few months on the ambulance, a trainee rides as the "fourth." He learns how patients are treated, what to avoid, and where various supplies are kept.

I was in the department for about a month before I went on any calls. I didn't yet know anyone on the ambulance crew and they didn't know me. In addition, I didn't understand what I was supposed to do on the ambulance. I would hear the siren going off and just sit there wondering if I should respond or not. Tommy Stasiak told me that eventually I would have to go, but I didn't feel ready. Then one day, the siren sounded and off I went. I got to the firehouse, climbed in the back of the ambulance and a rather large, unfriendly-looking man who I hadn't bumped into yet, glared at me and asked, "Who the hell are you?" I had some explaining to do before we took off. As it turned out, the ambulance wasn't needed on that call. We were turned back before we had even gone a mile, but the important fact for me was that I had actually gone on a call. It was a moral victory of sorts.

When responding to fires and EMS calls, you never know what is going to happen and you never know how you'll react. Each call is so unique that years later the firefighters will remember it as the "Church Fire," "High School Fire," or "Austin Road Crash," as if it were some event that the whole world should be aware of. Whatever the situation, when the truck pulls up to a good working structure fire, or the ambulance races up to an overturned, smoking vehicle, the men and women who answer those calls have to be ready to make a difference.

Sartre formed much of his philosophy from his life experience. When he was young, he studied philosophy at the Sorbonne and specialized in German thought. Then, suddenly, the German army was marching through the streets of Paris and French life would never be the same again. He found himself an intellectual in a defeated nation. So he wrote books about a person's choices even when it seems that he or she has no choices. He thought that we always have options. We can choose to make that new beginning.

The day I arrived at the firehouse, I was born again. The awards of my past life in the university wouldn't help me at a fire or rescue call. No matter what we do for a living, all firefighters are the same inside a fire. Fire is a great equalizer. It will seek us out and show us what is in our hearts. When the temperature gets high enough, all will be revealed. When the heat and the pressure are the greatest, all of our worst fears and most noble aspirations will have a chance to play themselves out. In those dark and smoky places there is ample opportunity for both cowardice and courage. Some great thinkers believed that gold is a metaphor for the human soul. The heat of the fire will eliminate the impure and leave only the gold. It must go through those transitions that ensure its purity. Similarly, the Bible tells us "gold is born in the furnace of affliction."

There are many junctures in peoples' lives when they feel stuck or in some kind of rut. For some people that rut dictates the rest of their lives. They settle in and stay there. But once in a while someone sees the opportunity to renew the whole business of living. This is the chance to start all over again. When I walked into the firehouse, I left my essence as a "professor" behind. I had to find myself all over again. I had to discover what was in my heart.

4

Education, or there are many ways to learn

What is truly remembered is written on the heart.

Scottish Proverb

As I grow older, I am often amazed how the same lessons that eluded me in my youth still elude me today. Sometimes I wonder how we learn one lesson but not another. I wonder why one person seems to learn from their mistakes while another just repeats the same things all over again. It is a mystery because education is not just about the educating our intellect; it is about the heart as well.

Jean-Jacques Rousseau wrote about education in the 1750's. Rousseau was a wild, free soul who had been abandoned at an early age. He educated himself and went on to become one of the most influential European thinkers of his day. Because he was self- educated, his ideas were eccentric and sometimes considered dangerous. Rousseau's most important contribution to education was the idea that all real learning must be guided by the interest of the student, that people cannot be forced to learn against their will. Rousseau believed that education should be the choice of the learner, not the teacher.

Unlike the regular schooling most of us go through, firefighting was something that I had chosen. My imagination had been fired by stories I had heard and pictures I had seen. As Rousseau knew, education should be practical but it also has to appeal to the heart. My education as a firefighter truly began with my first serious fire and it came as a great shock to me. I had been in the department for a few months but hadn't yet gone to any big fires. I didn't know if I was ready. Then one day I found myself swept up into one.

It was one of those beautiful days in the middle of April. The sun was shining in a cloudless blue sky and the trees were turning green. The daffodils had withered but the tulips were still in their glory. It happened to be one of my days off from teaching at Mercy College and I was down at the firehouse chatting with Walt Swarm. He was explaining how the pump on the fire truck worked when the big siren on the pole outside the firehouse started to sound. Walt leaned over and listened to the monitor as heavy smoke was being reported on F…. Terrace, not far from the firehouse. Walt looked up, chomping on a cigar, his face resembling the bull dog on his Mack Truck baseball cap, and said, "Well, today you're gonna learn about fire fightin'!" He laughed a kind of laugh that made me very nervous.

I knew I would probably be needed because it was a weekday and volunteer firefighters were going to be in short supply. Walt got in the cab of the attack rig. I jumped on the back of the truck and hung on as he pulled the big diesel outside. Walt turned on the flashing red lights. I climbed up onto the top of the truck and began to put on my gear, which was draped over the rails of the hose bed. As I buttoned my coat, the siren began to scream again and I listened as the dispatcher got more excited.

"Multiple calls are coming in for a confirmed working structure fire; a child may be trapped in the house!"

As I tried to button my coat, my hands were trembling and I could feel my whole body shaking. Cars came screeching into the parking lot with their blue lights flashing and their headlights on. People started running toward the truck and jumping on board. Tommy Stasiak climbed onto the hose bed and the truck began to rumble and lurch forward. Tony Luccaro was running after the truck, trying to catch up. Tony is forty years old, works as a social worker and talks with a real New York City accent. He loves to argue and loves to fight fires. He is short and looks a little like Al Pacino. Walt was getting up a head of steam when Tony leaped onto the back step and began climbing up onto the top of the truck. Walt turned on the siren and began to pull the air-horn.

Tommy Stasiak pointed up over the trees at a pillar of black smoke that was beginning to form near Kirk Lake, beyond the Red Mills Market. Working in prison for a decade has given Tommy a certain colorful manner in his speech.

"Buckle up rookie, you're gonna get warm today!" He laughed.

In our fire department, most members don't have their own fire-fighting gear. Only a few have their own equipment issued them and they keep it in a gear bag in the trunk of their cars. All of the other gear is kept on the trucks, lined up on the top of the hose bed where we can grab it and get dressed. So when a group of excited firefighters gets up on the hose bed and starts grabbing gear, sizes sometimes are not the first thing on anyone's mind. I put on boots that didn't fit, a coat that was too small, and a helmet that was too big, but at that moment I wasn't paying too much attention to little details like that. My heart was pounding and my mind was racing. What would we find? What was going to happen? What is it really like to be inside a fire? In a few minutes, all of those questions would be answered, but more importantly, I would find out how I would react inside a real fire. This was not a drill. This was not fake smoke. This was what real firefighters wait for.

As the truck rolled down Hill Street, we could smell the smoke. Tommy looked at Tony and me, figuring out how to tackle this job with limited resources.

"When we get there, Tony, you and whoever is in the front seat do a search, I'll back you up with the hose line, and the rookie will be my backup." Stasiak didn't use my name. I had not earned that honor yet. But when he said "the rookie" I knew what he meant.

There was no time to say "no." There was no more time for hesitation. It had all become very simple; in five minutes, my education as a firefighter would begin in earnest. In the space of a few hours I would either be a real firefighter or I would never show my face at the firehouse again. I had read the books and watched the tapes about fire fighting, but now it was to be hands-on experience. Today my education as a novice firefighter would be complete. As the old-time firefighters would say, this was "the real thing."

The truck turned the corner with its lights flashing and siren wailing. The fire was blowing out onto the street and a crowd from the neighborhood was gathered in the road. The truck rolled to a stop. There, just fifty feet away, was a house with fire licking out of the windows and smoke pouring into the sky. I could feel the heat the second my feet hit the ground.

"My God," I thought, "what have I gotten myself into?"

The fire itself was eye-catching. Terrifying and destructive as it is, a fire is also a phenomenon of beauty and fascination. It was the deepest hues of red and orange, with smoke that was as black as a moonless night. The fire danced and waved, filling the air with crackling and popping sounds. There it was, breathing, eating and daring us to approach. It was so hot it was hard to look at directly when I got close.

Walt and Tony were already off the truck. We put on our air bottles and adjusted the masks on our faces. Walt was yelling for us to hurry up because it seemed there were fifty important jobs to be done and none of them was started. Tony ran to the front door with an axe in his hand and disappeared into the hot blackness. As I watched him vanish, I felt my stomach turning somersaults. Tommy had pulled the hose to the front door and was crouching there. He waved for me to follow him. I looked at Walt Swarm, who had become a guru to me in the first few weeks I was in the department. Walt frowned.

"Get movin' rookie! What do we have to do, give ya' a written invitation?"

I ran up behind Tommy Stasiak and crouched behind him. The heat of the building was pouring out at us. I felt an overwhelming sense of panic, a combination of heat, suffocation, confusion, and claustrophobia, and I was gasping rapidly for breath. Despite all of the screaming and the sirens from the next arriving truck, I could still hear my heart pounding in my ears. Suddenly the limp hose stiffened as water pressure gave us the signal to go.

I will never forget what happened next. It forever changed my life and all that has happened since. Tommy was creeping toward the door. I knew what I had been taught. Tony was already inside and we had to go in and protect him with the hose during his search. For an instant there, in that heat and confusion, I hesitated. Suddenly I felt a sharp pain and I was moving forward, propelled by a force from behind me. I had gotten a good kick in my rear. Close to my ear I heard Walt Swarm's cantankerous, unmistakable voice, "Not next week, NOW!"

Before I knew what hit me, I was an inch behind Tommy Stasiak on the other side of the door. There was only blackness and the sound of my own breathing. I was hanging on to the tail of Tommy's coat with all of my strength. We crawled forward. The claustrophobia and the heat were overwhelming. Inside most structure fires, firefighters can't see anything. The smoke is so dark and dense that they must blindly feel their way forward, bumping into tables, chairs, and walls. Because they can't see, they don't know what they will find, where they are, or—most dangerously—which way they came in. It was okay for Tommy and me because we had the hose. If we got confused, we could always put the nozzle down and follow the hose back out to the truck. Tony was in there using all of his senses and feeling for victims, trying not to fall down stairs and hoping the floor hadn't fallen in right in front of him as he groped forward. We pressed on into the smoke and blackness. So far, there was no Tony, no victim, and no fire. There was only darkness and heat.

We turned a corner and suddenly the room exploded in reds, yellows, and whites, as flames licked the ceiling and rolled over our heads. We ducked and closed our eyes for a second as the freight train above us passed over. Tommy opened up the nozzle and began to put out the flames while I hung on to his coat for dear life. At one point I pulled myself next to his ear and yelled, "Shouldn't we be getting some relief soon?"

He patted me on the helmet and said in a muffled voice, "Take it easy pal; you're in good hands!"

I looked and saw the fire rolling on the ceiling above us. "Tommy, it's gonna roll over us and cut off our exit. We got to get out!"

He didn't say a word, he just kept spraying the hose. Tommy tracked the fire wherever it hid. We advanced into the flames and poured on the water until the steam was so thick that we couldn't see our hands in front of our faces. We forged on, taking every inch from that fire. Breathing heavily, I squinted and tried to stay as close to Tommy as I could. Suddenly I heard the alarm on my mask go off, a muffled clicking, warning me that I had just a few minutes of good air left. When that alarm goes off, it's time to get out and let somebody else take a turn.

I tapped Tommy on the shoulder and pointed at my mask. He had been around long enough to know what that meant. At that point, Tony passed us on his way out. Tommy set down the nozzle and we followed the hose line back outside.

By the time we got out, reinforcements had come and several firefighters were bottled up and ready to relieve us. I pulled off my mask and inhaled deeply. I cannot tell you what a pleasure that was. I'd never enjoyed the shining sun, the cloudless sky, and the cool fresh air so much! I was soaking wet from the hose spray and I had been sweating heavily for about twenty minutes. As I walked back to the truck, I staggered. Tommy caught me and I saw Walt Swarm give me a look of disgust.

"If you're gonna be a firefighter, ya can't be faintin' every time somebody lights a match!"

I sat down on the running board of the truck. Walt was watching the pump gauges as water was pulsing through the hoses into the fire. The whir of the pump and the pulse of the water through the hoses was a kind of music that Walt knew well. Tony came over to us drinking a can of soda.

"Good news—the kid got out before we got here."

After a few minutes, Tommy looked around. He looked back at me and pointed to the rescue truck that carries our spare air bottles.

"What do you say you and me get a fresh bottle and head back in?"

I smiled because I had realized something that day. After Walt had abruptly increased my courage with a well-placed kick and I found myself inside the fire, I had liked it. It's hard to explain, but there was something about being there—inside the fire—that was as exciting and dramatic as anything I'd ever experienced. We had stood inside an oven and not backed out. We had stood in a place that many people would never know. We had seen something few people would ever see. We were doing something heroic and good. There was the satisfaction of keeping your ground when every fiber in your body wanted you to bail out and run. If Walt hadn't given me a little encouragement, I might not have gone. But he did, I did, and those actions had forever changed my life. In a sense I've never wanted to leave a fire since that time. There inside the fire, with the nozzle spraying and my emotions on overload, I found an exhilaration beyond words.

I remember hearing a legend about the salamander told by Pliny the Elder. Pliny wrote that the salamander goes to the hottest part of the furnace to mate and the coldness of its body extinguishes the fire. The salamander later became an important image in the Middle Ages. One thinker believed that salamanders were beings of pure fire that could pass through walls. In the Bible, the salamander was compared to the three young Hebrews in the book of Daniel who were thrown into the fire by the king of Babylon but did not burn. Salamanders were later compared to Christ descending into Hell. Being impervious to fire, they went where others feared to tread.

Tommy and I bottled up and went back to the door. The fire was under control now. A lot of overhaul, salvage, and cleanup needed to be done. We went to work.

A few hours later we were back at the firehouse. The trucks were a mess. The wet, dirty hose was all stretched out in the parking lot. The air bottles were being refilled. Our faces were smudged and our clothes were soaked. We hung our coats and helmets in the sun to let them dry.

Our lieutenant had ordered some pizza and soda. We sat around and talked about where the fire had been, what we had done right, and what we could have done better. After a little while, Tommy, Tony Luccaro, and I drifted into the Red Mills Pub. We ordered an ice-cold pitcher of beer. I remember the radio was on. It was the Searchers doing *Needles and Pins*. The music reminded me of those sock hops I had gone to in high school. I thought of those old cars, my long lost friends, and the smile of my high school sweetheart. That song brought back memories of an easier and simpler time in my life. I was more relaxed at that moment, sitting there with Tommy and Tony, than I had been in a long time. I sipped my beer and we talked. I felt a sense of belonging I had not known in a long time. Somehow it seemed as if I had come home.

Jean Jacques Rousseau spent much of his life wandering through Europe. He traveled far and wide and I think that's what made him appreciate the simple things. He realized that learning, real learning, impresses the mind in a way that it will never forget. It awakens the imagination, and not just the intellect. It makes us hungry for more knowledge. Real education opens our minds and hearts at the same time.

My introduction to the world of fire had come suddenly and without warning. I was hesitating at that door when Chief Swarm made the decision for me. I seriously doubt that Walt Swarm had read much Rousseau. But as I hesitated at the door of that fire, he knew just how to make an impression on me, and not just on my mind.

5

Attention to Details, or how to focus on what is right in front of you

To see the world in a grain of sand and eternity in an hour.

William Blake

Sunday mornings can be depressing. Some people bring home a newspaper or two and watch the television news images of war, poverty and crime. They sit and drink their coffee, read the news, and get angry. They see the big picture and wonder why it does not change. Instead of paying attention to the details all around them, they set their eyes on things far away that they can't control. They read, they feel powerless, and nothing changes.

That's not what happens on Sunday mornings at the firehouse in my town. Every Sunday morning for the past half century, the Mahopac Falls Volunteer Fire Department has inspected, tested, and cleaned its emergency vehicles. I've been told that, although the attendance has been a little sparse from time to time, the firefighters haven't missed a Sunday—not on Pearl Harbor Day in 1941, not on the weekend that JFK was assassinated in 1963, and not even on New Year's Day—for fifty years.

No matter what goes on in the rest of the world, the fire trucks and ambulances have to be in tiptop shape if there is an emergency. Every single item on every single vehicle has to be there and work well. It's true that some weeks in Mahopac Falls the fire trucks don't roll from one Sunday to the next. They sit there all red and shiny with their chrome polished and gauges sparkling just waiting until they're needed.

Occasionally during the week some of the old-timers take a look under the hood of one of the trucks to see if the hoses and clamps are all right, test the alternator or inspect some particular piece of equipment. The firefighters check, double check, and recheck every single light, ladder, and hose because any one of these items could be the crucial one in that moment of life and death that most firefighters come to experience sooner or later. All of the preparation, the checking, and the inspecting are in readiness for a moment when a fire is raging out of control and each link in the chain must be strong and reliable.

When I first came to the firehouse, I was amazed at how quiet many of the firefighters were, and how much time they spent on their trucks and equipment. There is a regular Sunday morning crew that spends time down at the firehouse. They drink coffee, eat jelly doughnuts and chat while they do their weekly truck check. There is a religious regularity to this place. The trucks have to be done. The firefighters all know that the next fire could be at one of their houses.

Walt Swarm is a great believer in these inspections. His white Chevy pick-up truck can be found parked at the firehouse a good part of the time. You won't see Walt when you walk in. He's usually on his back on a creeper, one of those little platforms with wheels, under one of the old Mack trucks. He is either fixing a drive shaft or checking the brakes. Being retired, he has the time to putter. A few weeks ago, he yelled at me that some wires had been dragging under a truck and he had had to tape them to the chassis. He asked why I hadn't noticed it. I wanted to explain that I hadn't gotten under that particular truck in a few weeks, but he didn't give me the chance. Walt keeps us on our toes, whether we like it or not.

Walt knows that at any minute we can find ourselves in a situation where a small equipment malfunction will suddenly look very large. In the lifetime he's spent at the Falls, he's known many of these moments. These are times when being attentive to details pays off. He knows that at any minute, the time can come when a firefighter's preparation is tested.

In firefighters' language, that moment has a rather complicated technical name: it's called a "confirmed fully involved structure fire." When many fires are first called in, they are called "possible" because the call could be a prank call or false alarm. But when a police officer or fire officer at the scene calls it in, it is "confirmed." It is also called a "working structure fire," which means that the fire department will be working at it for a while. A "structure fire" is a fire in a building. It could be a house, a barn, a garage, or a shed. The structure fires that firefighters battle most aggressively are house fires. In these fires, they take the hose line inside the fire to try to save someone's home. "Fully involved" means that the fire is not confined to a single room but has spread through the entire house.

In most small rural fire departments, an occasion when someone's house may be totally lost and the lives of the firefighters are at risk does not come every day. It's an event that firefighters anticipate and prepare their trucks and equipment in readiness for. Fire doesn't take Christmas or Thanksgiving off. It doesn't know any holidays or seasons. Because fire arrives suddenly and without warning, firefighters practice for it and they work towards it, even if it comes only a few times a year. Like sheepdogs on a farm with no sheep, they sit, talk, tinker, and fuss. They wait and wait and wait for the siren to sound.

It is probably hard to know what it is like to be a volunteer firefighter or EMS volunteer if you haven't been one or lived with one. Think about living a life when at any second of any day, your pager could go off, telling you someone is trapped in a fire or choking and needs your help. Imagine lying in bed on a relaxing Saturday night and some part of you knows that at any second that alarm could ring and rip you out of your sleepy world. Imagine knowing that at any time you could be called and be in harm's way.

Many people join the fire department and find out that this sacrifice is too great. Many relationships have felt the strain of that commitment. A lot of energy is used in its service. It is a commitment so great I sometimes wonder myself how anyone could make it. Volunteer firefighters never can relax the way other people do. Some secret part of their mind is always waiting for those tones to go off and send them into another life.

At Mahopac Falls, one long blast of the siren signals an ambulance call and three blasts signals a fire. In every small village and town in America right now, there are people—barbers, plumbers, insurance salespeople, and butchers—waiting and listening for these sounds. Over at the Red Mills Market, Tony the butcher will come to the alarm. In the school, the custodians will leave their tasks and head to the firehouse. From the local florist, three of our members will drop what they are doing and head on over. Mothers will leave their housework and truckers will do a U turn and start heading for the Falls.

Years ago, there was only a fire-gong that would be clanged and everyone within earshot would respond. Like other mementos of traditions at the firehouse, the firefighters could never bear to throw it away when its useful life ended. That old fire gong is still hanging in front of the Mahopac Falls Volunteer Fire Department. When I asked what it was still doing there, an old firefighter told me that they kept it in case of an emergency. Today, firefighters carry pocket pagers, but they still sound the siren for every fire and ambulance call. When the siren sounds over and over again and the call comes out over the pager for more manpower and help from other departments, a firefighter knows that something big is happening. Throughout towns in America, the siren blast signals a call for help in time of need.

When the siren does sound at the Falls and the pocket pagers kick on, there is a scramble towards the trucks. Buttons are pressed to raise the electronic overhead doors. Keys are turned in the ignitions of trucks that must start up without any hesitation and run for hours until the blaze is over. In many rural fire departments, to prevent them from being turned off and not starting again, trucks are never shut off until they are back in the "barn" or firehouse. Many of our trucks are diesels and are sensitive to cold weather. The moment the trucks pull out onto the pavement, cars with their blue lights flashing are pulling into the parking lot from all directions. Firefighters with their bags of equipment are scurrying towards the trucks. The trucks have their flashers going and engines gunning. Nobody wants to miss the first truck out, which is called the "attack truck." Those in the cab of the attack truck will be fully dressed and have their air bottles on when they get to the fire. If it is a "working structure fire," or a "worker," they will be called upon to take the first hose line and perhaps go inside a maze of black smoke and licking flame. This is what they prepare for and dream about.

The air bottles must be full and working, the hose functional, and the truck able to supply water. If any of this equipment isn't operating properly, the consequences can be severe. It is in preparation for these dangerous encounters that the apparatus sits in readiness and all the care is taken with the trucks and the equipment on them.

In Mahopac Falls most fires aren't "working structure fires." Some of the fires that get called in are car fires, burning mail-boxes, burning trees, and other small incendiary incidents. (For instance, we once had a call for a tree on fire at three a.m. One of our officers got on the radio to say he was responding to the tree fire. It turned out that a prankster had set someone's little hedge on fire. For a long time after this, we joked that the unfortunate officer who had gone to the bush fire had one thing in common with Moses: both responded to the call of the burning bush.)

The Mahopac Falls fire district receives about 500 ambulance calls a year, more than one a day. It has two ambulances and a rescue truck, and in the case of something as serious as a bad car accident or a school bus collision, everything rolls. The ambulance calls can be anything from a cut finger to life-threatening events like a heart attack or severed limb. Those are calls that the members never forget.

Each of the two ambulances carries 174 different items on it. They include scissors, clamps, masks, and bandages of various sizes. There are different sizes of oxygen cylinders, ace bandages, cutting tools, flares, and scores of other items. To remind us of the importance of every piece of equipment, we have a saying that you never need all 174 on each call, only the one you forgot to restock last Sunday. Each ambulance, or "rig," has a lieutenant who is responsible for keeping it supplied and in good mechanical order. If anything is wrong mechanically or if any of the 174 different items are in low supply, the lieutenant may get a midnight phone call at home to come down to the firehouse and refit the rig. If a mirror is cracked, a windshield is dirty, or the oxygen is low, he or she will hear about it.

Tony Luccaro has been riding the ambulance every Sunday night for the past twenty years. He doesn't ever sleep through a call and can be counted on to make it to the rig first. He lives about a mile from the firehouse and so gets there quickly. If he jumps in the ambulance at three a.m. and has a hard time seeing through the windshield, or notices that the gas-tank is half rather than three-quarters full, he'll let the offender know. "After all," he once said, "these are people's lives we're talking about here."

Some of the Emergency Medical Technicians who ride the rigs come down and check them out before they are on night duty, which lasts from ten p.m. to six a.m.

The same attention to detail is given to the fire trucks. Every lieutenant has a truck, and he or she has to know which bulbs are out, which scratches are where, and who nicked what. With trucks currently costing more than $250,000 each, it's no wonder that each one is pampered and constantly inspected. Every missing bolt must be attended to. Every week the trucks are polished, the wheel wells are hosed down, and the windshields are made transparent.

This attitude towards the trucks is much like the attitude of Zen monks tending to their temple. The monks' purpose in constant polishing the floor is not so much a polishing of things as an emptying of the mind. It's a way of keeping so busy that they forget themselves. The mind that is freed from anxiety and worry is like a calm pool or clean mirror that reflects images clearly and without shadow. In Zen practice, monks are taught to look at and enjoy the world as a mirror does, not questioning, not distorting, not grasping.

The gleaming trucks at our firehouse are like the cleanly polished surfaces of a Zen temple. It took me a while to understand that, in maintaining their trucks, Walt and the other firefighters are caring for themselves. By giving themselves over to those trucks, they forget their troubles. They become a part of a tradition and a discipline—like Zen. By being a link in an unbroken chain of service, they become more than simply themselves.

On the other hand, sloppiness with fire equipment reflects an inner inattentiveness. One time, on a visit to another firehouse with Tony Luccaro and Walt Swarm, I noticed that not only were their trucks dirty and the hose not racked on the truck properly but there was a pool of oil on the floor beneath the truck engine. Walt stared at that pool of oil and looked at me. He shook his head sadly. I knew what he was thinking, and I wondered if the engine might not be up to the task when the ignition key was turned on.

The way people deal with objects in their environment can be quite revealing. Firefighters and EMS people frequently find themselves in other people's bedrooms, bathrooms, and basements when they are not expected. We are uninvited guests. Imagine fifteen strangers suddenly standing in your bedroom or going through your basement. How would you feel right then? Firefighters and EMS personnel spend time in other people's houses, houses where misfortunes and disasters have struck. Some of those houses are not as neat as they could be. It encourages the firefighters to keep their own houses in better shape. Years of seeing how other houses looked at four a.m. have made them careful.

When a good "worker" happens, you see which trucks have been maintained and which ones need more work. I remember one fire we had in a basement. The truck pulled up to a good working structure fire at around two a.m. and the firefighters pulled the first attack line off. I was in the cab of the second truck and was at the door when they were stretching the line. The flashing red truck lights lit up the darkness and there was activity everywhere. The smoke was spilling out of the front door and some of the windows into the cool April night. Tommy Stasiak was there at the door organizing the attack. Suddenly, something happened. Tony Luccaro, the man on the nozzle, stood back and Tommy Stasiak took the line and extinguished the fire.

After the fire was over, I met Tony outside. He explained to me that when he went to pull down his mask before he went into the building, he found that the straps were already pulled tight. The masks are supposed to be left with all of the straps loose so that firefighters can slip them on and then tighten them to get a good "seal." This prevents toxic smoke and gases from choking them. When Tony realized that the mask was not going to fit, he had to let someone else take his place as he stepped back to readjust the mask, forcing him to waste precious time. When firefighters are making an interior attack, there is no time for adjustments. They have to get inside or get out of the way. Tony is one of the most experienced and courageous firefighters we have in the department and he was disappointed at having to give up the nozzle. The one on the nozzle often gets credit for making a "good stop" by putting out a fire quickly. Tony lost that opportunity. "That was my stop!" he said afterwards. "Somebody should have checked that mask!"

On Sunday morning at the Falls, there are doughnuts and coffee for us. We eat and gossip while the trucks get done. Across the street at the Baptist Church, the bell can sometimes be heard tolling and the sound of hymn singing can sometimes be heard. We, at the firehouse, are singing a different hymn, a hymn to details, machines, and preparation.

When we are done, we put WHUD on the radio, pour some coffee and just socialize.

We can sit there and discuss the weather or politics as we listen to the Four Seasons sing *Dawn.*

In Buddhism there is a doctrine of "no-mind." This means forgetting yourself and becoming absorbed in the world around you. This is achieved in Zen by focusing attention on details. When Zen monks walk, they watch where they place their feet. When they clean a bowl, it must be spotless and empty. When they meditate, they try to do it with all of their heart so that their mind is as clear as a bell ringing in an empty sky. There's a Zen saying: "The greatest sin is inattention." In Zen, the idea is to forget the big picture and pay attention to the details.

On Sunday mornings at the Falls, the trucks are pulled out onto the pavement and washed. Inside, the floor is swept and scrubbed. The floor is done by all of us, including Art Brady, Charlie Locke, Tommy Stasiak, Tony Luccaro, and Walt Swarm. By noon, the trucks are so shiny that they reflect everything around them like a red mirror. For a few hours, once a week, we can forget our problems and lose ourselves in the polished reflection of a mirror. At that moment there is no "I" or "you," but a dance where one loses oneself in the music of humming engines and purring pumps.

Details can be important. Let me tell you my favorite story about how a little detail can have a big impact. I remember one time we had a fire and everything was in disarray afterwards.

One of the new members washed off the masks from the air packs and left them to dry outside the firehouse. As fate would have it, we had another fire the same night. We rushed into the firehouse around one a.m. and the trucks roared out with us onboard half asleep. It was only when we were about three blocks from the fire we realized we had air bottles but no masks. They had been left drying outside the firehouse. Fortunately, we were the third truck in so this was not the disaster it could have been. But it taught that rookie an important lesson about which details should be attended to. That whole operation could have ended because of an innocent, simple mistake.

I don't know if the world has an essence. Perhaps we can never know the "big picture" of why we were born or why the world is the way it is. But there is something I do know. Each detail we come across is a mirror in which we can see ourselves, a mirror where perhaps, if we pay attention to what we are doing, we can focus on the present moment and truly be at peace with whatever we are doing.

6

Heroism, or realizing there are many ways to be a hero

Heroism—that is the disposition of a man who aspires to a goal compared to which he himself is wholly insignificant. Heroism is the good will to self-destruction.

Freidrich Nietzsche

Heroes are found in every culture and in every age. The hero goes where ordinary mortals fear to tread and does so with boldness that excites imagination and awe. In many myths, the hero has special weapons and protection. Often, as the story progresses, the hero is stripped, one by one, of the magic helmet, belt of invisibility, winged shoes, invincible armor, and singing sword. Typically, in the end, the hero finds himself vulnerable in the cave of the fire-breathing dragon, with only his wits and courage to protect him. The design of these myths suggests that, in addition to physical heroism, life reveals a deeper inner heroism as well.

In Greek mythology, a hero often overreaches by being too proud. This was the sin Greeks called "hubris." Jason, who sought the Golden Fleece, Oedipus, who searched for the truth, or Prometheus, who attempted to bring the gift of fire, all suffered even though they were the noblest and best. Oftentimes the hero was the offspring of both god and mortal. But this divine parentage was not enough to protect them from the balance of fate that holds us all in check. Even the offspring of the gods failed in certain tasks.

The Greek historian, Herodotus, told tales about heroes. One such tale is so compelling and powerful that it has been retold again and again. It is a story that has inspired generations that have heard it. It's the story of a hopeless effort and ultimate courage in the face of incredible odds. It's the story of three hundred Spartans sacrificing their lives to save their people and protect their honor.

Twenty-four hundred years ago, Greece was not a unified country. It was made up of many small city-states that were constantly at war with each other. This constant internal squabbling left the Greeks weak and vulnerable. Meanwhile, to the east, where Iran is now, lay the great Persian Empire, ruled by a cruel and ruthless tyrant named Xerxes (pronounced Zerk zees). Xerxes wanted Greece under his dominion. He assembled an army so large, Heroditus tells us it took two weeks to pass a single location. Some accounts place the size of the army between one and four million soldiers. A feared and brutal unit known as "The Immortals" led them. As they marched, they destroyed the territories they occupied and used up all of the food and supplies.

To enter Greece, Xerxes's huge and seemingly unstoppable juggernaut had to march through a narrow pass that the Greeks called Thermopile. In that pass stood the three hundred Spartans whose aim was to slow down the Persian forces for at least a few days—enough time to give the other Greek city-states a chance to organize their defense. Although the Greek force at the pass was originally seven thousand, six thousand were sent home. Knowing the odds against them, the leader of the Spartans kept only those who knew there was no way out, sending even more home. The force remaining was small, only 300 men. The Spartans knew that the Persians had the largest army the world had ever known and they must have known there was little chance of a Spartan victory.

The three hundred Spartans believed that there would be reinforcements. But due to politics, the reinforcements never arrived. They were left, as we say, "holding the bag." Even though everything conspired against them, they carried themselves so nobly and with such courage that twenty-four hundred years later, their heroism is still remembered.

Although there were no survivors, Herodotus and other historians had the accounts of eyewitnesses who had left the day before and accounts of the Persians after the battle.

King Leonides was the Spartan leader. When the Persians arrived on the other side of pass, their army was so large that their night campfires stretched to the horizon. The Spartans must have known their fate when the battle began. Just before hostilities ensued, one of the Spartans was told that the Persian archers were so numerous that "their arrows would blot out the sun." With characteristic Spartan calm, one soldier replied, "Good, then we can fight in the shade."

Firefighters are often thought of as heroes. In some cities firefighters are called that city's "bravest." To run into a burning building when everyone else is running out does take a special kind of person. Firefighters also have dreams. They dream of that special moment when they do something that will be remembered for the rest of their lives. Moments that test one's physical courage in a fire don't come every day, so when they do happen, a firefighter has to take advantage of them. I had such a moment, but it turned out quite differently than I had always dreamed.

It happened on a summer morning. It was already a hot day, with all of those sounds in the air that sing the songs of late summer. The trees were green and the smell of grass and flowers drifted through the air. The crickets and the bees sang their symphonies in various keys.

I was sitting in my back yard with my morning coffee, listening to an aria from Mozart's *Magic Flute* on the radio when my pager suddenly tripped. It beeped so loud it startled me out of my drowsy meditation. On the other end I recognized our police dispatcher, Mike Johnson, giving us the scoop. "Smoke investigation on A…. Road." Mike has a slow and dreamy voice on the air. Mike is a big teddy bear of a guy who goes by the nickname "Taters" because of his fondness for French fries. No matter what the emergency, Sergeant Johnson never ever gives the impression that he is slightly interested.

I was closer to the scene than the firehouse, so I decided to head over to the area of the call and see what was happening. As I got closer, the pager tripped again. Now Mike Johnson was telling a different and more serious story: "Possible structure fire on A…. Road." Sure enough, as I came to the road and turned in, I saw that something was on fire. Black smoke was heavy in the air and I could smell the peculiar scent of a fire. The smell of a house fire is unmistakable. It is a dry woody smell that contains in it the odors of burning plastics and fabrics. There is a bitter smell that tells us many things are mixing together inside the fire.

I was the first one on the scene. No other firefighters or police had arrived yet. By this time I had been in the department long enough to be issued my own firefighting gear, which I always kept with me. I parked my car and opened the trunk. I took out my boots, coat, and fire helmet. As I raced to put them on, the neighbors began to appear, pointing at the house and yelling. The last thing I picked up was my forcible entry tool, a short crow bar with a hook on the end and a steel point that's used to break in doors or windows. It is about as long as a short sword and I always clutch it as I am approaching a burning building. Sometimes I think of that tool as my security blanket. As I walked up to the house, I noticed a car parked in the driveway, alerting me that someone might still be in the house. Many times, firefighters search a home to see if anyone is there. Like Socrates and Plato, we never assume. I got down beside the door and pulled on my gloves. On my radio I heard Tommy Stasiak's voice: "19-2-3 is en route to the structure fire on A…. Road with a full crew."

Listening I was sure I could hear Walt Swarm cursing at him in the background about something. It occurred to me that no matter how dangerous the situation, Walt always had the time and energy to cuss us out both coming and going from a fire. Reinforcements were on the way, but I didn't have the time or luxury to wait for them.

I tried to open the door, but it was locked. I felt the handle and it felt cool enough to go inside. (A hot door is a warning not to open it; it means there is a great amount of heat and possibly fire on the other side.) I forced open the door and ducked low. Immediately, smoke came pouring out. I didn't have my air bottle with me, and I was alone, so I would have to be very careful. I entered the house very slowly and began to inch my way forward, squinting in an effort to see. Although it was smoky, there was some limited visibility. I could feel the heat and I was coughing in the smoke as I crawled forward. The smoke was starting to roll lower, which meant the house was beginning to heat up. When a fire ignites, the smoke goes to the ceiling, where most of the heat and poison gases stay. As the fire continues to burn, the gases bank down and heat up the whole room. I still had some breathable air near the floor, but I had to stay low to get it. I also knew I was running out of time.

As I found my way into the living room of the small house, I noticed something on the sofa. I made my way over to it. There was a man lying unconscious on the sofa. I took off my gloves and felt for a pulse. The pulse was strong. My heart began to race. I had been in a few fires, and I had searched for "possible victims" before, but this was the first time I had ever found anyone. Just then, I heard the air horn and sirens of the fire truck and I knew that Stasiak and the others would soon be at the front door to help me. But it was getting hotter every second. Shortly, the smoke would be down low enough to take the good air away from me. I didn't have time to wait. I pulled the man off the sofa and began to pull him through the living room. He was large and felt like dead weight. As I dragged him along, every muscle in my body was straining. Being a college philosophy professor does not take too much physical effort. I sit and chat all day long. This means I sometimes am not in the best of shape. This wasn't helping me now. As I struggled, I backed into chairs and felt the rug slide under my feet, but I was determined to make it. Still coughing in the smoke, I grunted and pulled until I felt the exhilarating breath of fresh air blowing behind me. I had made it to the front door. I stood up, and with a final effort I brought the man over the threshold and laid him down next to the door outside. I pulled off my helmet. He was still breathing, so there was no need to start CPR. I collapsed on the ground in exhaustion.

Starting to recover, I looked up at the truck and saw the firefighters getting their equipment. As they pulled the hose up the driveway, I wasn't paying attention to the fire. I was lost in visions of the headlines of tomorrow's newspaper: "Professor Saves

Man in Burning Building," or, more simply, "Heroic Rescue." I even started to write the article in my mind.

Before I could finish the first sentence, I heard a groan. The man I had rescued was waking up and glaring at me angrily. He was a rather tough-looking character and his rough demeanor made me nervous right off the bat.

"Who the hell are you?" he growled.

I explained I was a firefighter and that I had just rescued him from his own house.

"Who said you could come in my house? Did you take anything?"

He was now starting to get downright nasty. Then I noticed he had the word "death" tattooed between the knuckles of his right hand. As I looked at his face I noticed that he had one glass eye and a mean expression. I was beginning to understand that this was one rough character that did not appreciate my "heroic" rescue. This wasn't turning out to be the triumph I had planned.

The next thing I knew, Tommy Stasiak was standing next to me. As a corrections officer for many years, he was more accustomed to dealing with this kind of tough customer than I was. He had obviously been listening to the conversation and looked at me with a smile.

"Doctor Frank, Do you want to introduce me to your friend?"

This infuriated the hostile man even more and he launched into a rage against us both. He said we had no right to enter his house and no right to yank him around. He started to complain about his neck feeling bad where he had been dragged. I was getting more nervous every second. Suddenly this fellow was up and in my face, screaming and pointing at his neck. Stasiak started to step in when one of our local police officers approached us. Apparently our customer was an old and familiar acquaintance of the police. He had expressed himself to them frequently so they knew him well.

As the police officer approached, the man pushed me. Tommy jumped in between us. In a minute, the policeman had the man on the ground and was cuffing him while he screamed profanities, threatening to sue me and take every cent the fire department had. I looked back at the truck and caught Walt Swarm's eye. He was shaking his head in disgust. At that moment he was pumping the truck and had other business to attend to. I looked at Tommy, who had a grin as big as a harvest moon. I smiled too. "OK, Stasiak, we have a fire to fight."

While we had been arguing with our victim, the firefighters had taken a hose into the house and knocked the fire down. It was a fairly simple deal to fight the fire and figure out what had happened. Our friend had been drinking, left some food cooking on the stove, and then passed out. The food burned, the pot melted, the flame spread, and the fire was climbing up the wall and onto the ceiling. It took only a few minutes to get the fire under control. Now there was the job of making sure there were no hot spots left to rekindle. As we walked through the kitchen, Tommy stopped at the kitchen table where a bottle of vodka sat next to a box of corn flakes and a bowl. Tommy picked up the bowl with a corrections officer's suspicious eye, sniffed it, and put it down.

"Vodka over cornflakes?" I asked him.

He smiled. "The breakfast of champions, pal."

We went outside into the hot summer sun. I remember there was a flower garden in the yard across the street full of marigolds and asters. Red roses climbed behind it on a green thorn bush. Tommy and I went over to the attack truck and sat on the back step with Walt Swarm. Somebody handed me a bottle of water. I took a big drink while coughing from the smoke I had inhaled. I was exhausted and dehydrated. Walt Swarm looked at me.

"Ya happy pa'fessor?"

I didn't look him in the eye.

"Ya get beat up, ya get Stasiak in trouble, and now we're gonna get sued? How are ya gonna explain this one?"

I would have answered, but I was too demoralized. I could see Stasiak looking at Swarm. In a minute both of them were laughing. In another minute I was laughing too. We put the hose back on the truck, a procedure called "racking hose." There is an art to racking hose and it must be done with care and attention. The hose must be laid in such a way that it pulls off fast and clean when it needs to come off the truck. We got the truck back in shape and headed back to the firehouse.

When we returned to the station, other firefighters were pulling in. Walt couldn't wait to tell them the story. In my moment of glory, things had gone wrong. I knew the members would kid me for a long time about what had happened. Kidding plays an important role in the fire department. It's a way many firefighters have of expressing their feelings indirectly. They don't spend much time telling each other that they love each other or complaining that life lacks meaning. They have other ways of expressing their feelings, and kidding is one of them. It allows firefighters to playfully enjoy each other without bringing in any emotional baggage.

A few hours later, Tommy and I were at the diner with our usual cup of coffee. I was embarrassed and disappointed.

"You know, Tommy, I thought I had it made. I was already thinking of the headlines."

Stasiak drank his coffee. "Thinking up headlines? Like 'Doctor Frank Rescues Man'"?

"Something like that."

Stasiak was laughing, and I was laughing too.

When I arrived at the firehouse the next morning, Walt Swarm and Tony Luccaro were drinking coffee. The radio was tuned to WHUD and DJs, Mike and Casey, were playing Leslie Gore singing *Maybe I Know*.

Walt greeted me. "Well, Pa'fessor have you read the morning paper?"

I told him I hadn't. He held up the headline. "Man Brawls with Firefighters."

That was all I needed. Not the heroic story I had in mind, but a story nonetheless. It was a tale that would be told for a long time at the Mahopac Falls Volunteer Fire Department.

For three days the Spartans held off the Persian horde. But a Greek, hoping for financial reward, showed the Persians a secret path over the mountains to get behind the Greeks. Cut off from both sides, the Spartans fought bravely but were slaughtered. Not one survived. They had bought three precious days with their lives. They had resisted long enough to prevent Xerxes's army from advancing any farther and pouring into Europe. At the cost of their lives, the Spartans had saved their country from enslavement to the Persian Empire.

I have never been to Thermopile, but I have read that if you visit the site you will see two inscriptions. One is for all the Greeks. It says, "Here three hundred Spartans held off four million Persians." But there is another inscription, one just for the Spartans. It records the words of the Spartan King Leonides, who, when he knew his fate was sealed, selected one of his men to go back to Sparta and tell them what had happened. He wanted the Spartans to know that even though he had no reinforcements and there was no hope of victory or even survival, he would do his duty and stand his ground. These were his words: "Go tell the Spartans, we lie here obedient to our word."

Those words are carved into the rock wall. They stand as a monument to the human spirit. They are the marks of heroism. When there were just a few Spartans left, the Persian King Xerxes offered them their freedom if they would give him the body of their king, Leonides. They refused. It did not matter that they stood alone. It did not matter that no one else came to help. They kept their word. Near the pass, you can still see the Spartan burial mound. I have always thought it was fitting that they be buried at the place of that heroic battle and not back in Sparta, for it was there that their spirits shone most brightly.

At the Falls Firehouse, we don't talk too much about heroism. That word is too full of self-importance for down-to-earth people like Walt Swarm and Tommy Stasiak. Instead, they talk about making things better and leaving the world better at the end of every day. Being a hero doesn't always mean doing the unexpected or the unusual. It means that day in and day out a person does his or her best.

For a while, I thought I had had my big chance at heroism. I was five minutes away from firefighter heaven. But in my moment of heroism, the person I had rescued did not show the appreciation I had hoped for. I learned another lesson about heroism that day. When I began to ask myself what real heroism is, I began to realize there are many kinds of heroism. Yes, there is the heroism of the three hundred Spartans. But there is another, less well known kind. I learned that real heroism isn't just pulling somebody out of a burning building. It can be the way a person lives every day with grace and kindness. It can be a person who lives everyday with chronic pain. It can be a mother carefully giving herself over and over again for her children. It can be a person who works everyday at a job that makes the world a better place. There are people in my town who have quietly coached little league soccer for the Mahopac Sports Association every week for twenty years. Maybe real heroism is holding your temper or doing what's in your heart. Some heroism can be small and quiet. It can be precious and rare. Almost always it leaves no stone inscription that will last through the ages. It leaves its mark only on the human heart. That's where real heroism is found.

7

Dreaming, or how not to miss the important things in life

Dreams come true; without that possibility, nature would not incite us to have them.

John Updike

Some people live only in their dreams. They dream they are some place other than where they are. They dream about a different job, a different life, or about living in another place. They dream about money, romance, or adventure.

That's probably why television and movies are popular with so many people. When those screens are lit, viewers are transported out of their own world. They can spend a few hours living someone else's life.

Dreams have always fascinated people. In ancient times, it was thought that our dreams revealed the future or that the gods could speak to us through dreams in ways that our conscious minds would not accept. For a long time after the coming of Christianity, dreams were thought to be the province of the devil, bearing messages that were sometimes frightening and unclear. Even in philosophy, where reason and logic are so important, dreams have played a crucial part. Socrates was often guided by his dreams. Rene Descartes, famous for inventing a method of finding the truth by doubting every thing that could be doubted, got the idea from a dream he had one night.

In his book *Madame Bovary*, Gustave Flaubert wrote about a woman who dreamed of living another life. His heroine, Emma Bovary, finds life in her small town too dull, her real world much less fascinating than the world of her dreams and imagination. She longs for another life, a life where every moment is filled with intensity.

The secret lives of trucker Walt Swarm, or Tommy Stasiak, the corrections officer, are filled with the kind of intensity that Madame Bovary looked for. What they do fighting fires and saving people's lives can be more exciting than anything I could dream of.

When I'm teaching at school, I like to play the professor. My colleagues at Mercy College, like my friends at the firehouse, are interesting, but in a different way. I'm friendly with a professor of English poetry, another who is an expert in Jazz and Opera, and another who is an expert in Chinese History. We have wonderful conversations about a wide range of topics from Shakespeare's poetry to Italian opera to the political beliefs of Machiavelli. College life is unhurried and thoughtful. Many of the professors truly care about the young minds in their charge and work hard trying to shape lives. It can be a pleasant way to make a living.

While at the firehouse the drink of choice is beer, here at Mercy College, the professors often sit down for a cup of coffee with each other. I often have coffee with two friends in the English department, Joel and Howard. Our conversations are literate and fun. We may talk about a medieval poem such as the "Dream of the Rood" and explore all of its hidden meanings. We try to see how we can apply new interpretations to it. Howard is always working on a new scholarly article and often asks my advice. Together we think about the best ways to communicate our ideas. Conversation can be a wonderful thing for those who know the art.

But sometimes I can't wait until my office hours are over and class is finished. I can't wait to begin living my other life, the one that finds its way into my dreams. When I leave the college, I turn on my pager, my radio link with that secret life. When I'm teaching, I leave it in my car because I try to pay full and complete attention to what I am doing at that particular moment. When teaching, one should teach; when fighting a fire, one's mind should focus on that. When I drive off campus and begin the forty-minute commute home at the end of my teaching day, I turn on the pager so I'm "tuned in" to what's happening, to what might be needed, and to what might be about to happen.

One day, at about three o'clock on a Thursday in June, the siren began to scream. The call came over for a structure fire on A.... Road. Walt Swarm took the wheel of the attack truck, with Tommy Stasiak and me on board with him. Racing down the road, we heard Sergeant Mike Johnson, our sleepy-sounding police dispatcher, updating us: "Numerous phone calls coming in. The callers are reporting heavy concentrations of smoke. Confirmed working structure fire."

As always, Sergeant Johnson didn't sound too excited. I could imagine him saying those words, taking a sip of coffee, looking at his watch and thinking his shift would be over in a few minutes. But for us it was another matter.

As we reached the crest of the hill on Bullet Hole Road, we could see a plume of smoke. At that point, we knew we had a job to do. The truck rounded the corner and rolled up to an old farm-house with smoke pouring out of all the windows on the third floor. We jumped off the truck, grabbed the hose, and our tools. I made sure my air bottle was full and we entered the front door. We made it to the second floor where the smoke was really getting thick, but there was no heat.

Tommy Stasiak was close behind me as the other firefighters began to climb the stairs behind us. One of the firefighters was Camille Lapine. Camille works as a registered nurse when she is not volunteering. Camille is a young woman, black-haired, about five feet two inches tall and is also an EMT. Many of our EMTs spend more time in the ambulance than inside fires. Camille, however, loves to fight fires.

We moved, low to the ground, up to the third floor, but oddly there was still no heat, even though the smoke was so thick that we couldn't see. Heat is one way to find a fire when it can't be seen, but we were out of luck this time. A thought came to me and I turned to Tommy. "I think it might still be in a mattress or sofa. It hasn't broken out yet. Keep that nozzle ready; we're stuck pretty high up here and I don't want us to get in trouble!"

We began feeling around with our hands, opening doors, and tripping over clutter as we moved forward. Time was passing and my nerves were telling me that if we didn't come across the source of the smoke soon, the fire could break out and attack us with no warning. Suddenly a face appeared out of the smoke. It was Camille.

"I think I got it!" She pointed to the mattress in the corner. I felt it. It was warm. We had to get it out of the house fast because it could burst into flames at any moment. We also had to be careful. While there was not a lot of oxygen in the closed space we were in, if we gave it air, the fire could break out quickly and violently. The hose was down the hall and we didn't have time to wait for it. We opened the window as far as it would go, but the mattress wouldn't fit through the opening. I pointed to the window. "Camille, Tommy, take it out!"

While they smashed the frame and took out all of the broken glass, I could now see flames starting to peek out of the mattress. The fire was starting to break out; the rush of air was feeding it, and it was ready to flash to life and become much more dangerous. The three of us grabbed the mattress and shoved it out the window. The mattress flew down and landed just as it began to burn.

As the smoke cleared, Tommy looked at the wall. He's been in a lot of fires and knows their marks and signs. He pointed to the wall next to where the mattress had been. It was charred and hot to the touch. Just next to it was the window, surrounded by drapes that had been just about ready to catch fire when we arrived. Now, with the exception of a window frame, a mattress, and a fresh coat of paint, the family's possessions were saved. We had saved their yearbooks, their old checks, their wedding pictures, their photograph albums, and all of their treasures and memories.

We picked up our hoses and headed back to the Falls fire department. Back at the station, sodas and a pizza were waiting for us as we cleaned the tools and re-racked the hose. The oldies radio station was on and the trucks were parked outside, ready to be washed. The sky was sapphire blue. At one point I asked Tommy if he ever dreamed of a different life with other kinds of adventures and excitement. He grinned. "Man, haven't you had enough adventures for one day?"

I remember he once told me he didn't like most movies because they weren't as exciting as what happened to him in a typical week.

On the radio, the Duprees were singing *You Belong to Me*.

I guess I feel the same way Tommy does, although he's had more adventures than I have. I don't dream of being anyone else. Lately, I haven't felt the itch that used to be so strong in me. Before, no matter where I was, I always longed to be someplace else. Now I feel like I am home.

The radio played softly as we worked on the trucks. I have found that there's no need to travel far to find danger, romance, or adventure. They're happening around us all the time, but most people just never notice. Tonight, while you sleep, someone's life might be saved right in your neighborhood. In fact, this happens so often that it usually doesn't make the morning paper. Our local paper, *The Journal News*, doesn't even mention ambulance calls.

Tonight, fires will be fought, lives will be saved, children will be rescued, and tomorrow when the sun comes up, there will be no trace of what went on. It will be as if these events never happened. Tonight, an invisible network of radio signals will interlock fire departments all over America and connect thousands of bands of local heroes living secret lives that are sometimes so amazing that I ask myself, in the middle of night, whether it is real or I'm only dreaming.

I remember once being at a fire all night that ended just about dawn. I was dirty, my face was black, and I smelled of smoke. I had to go home, shower, put on my suit and tie, and go to work teaching a Greek philosophy class. I was complaining how tired I was. I guess I was looking for a shoulder to cry on. Well, Walt Swarm gave me one of those foul looks that old-time firefighters are famous for and gave me his views on my exhausted state.

"What are you complainin' about? Teachin'? That's not work! Hell, in my day we'd fight a fire all night and bale hay the next day! That's work!"

He stuck the cigar back in his mouth and started back to work on the truck. Walt isn't much of a dreamer; he has too many things to do.

Some people do and others dream. One thing I've learned is that our lives are something we decide how to live everyday. We can drag ourselves through them, hoping things will get better somewhere down the line or we can live fully and maybe even heroically. I've heard it said that "talk is cheap" and that "actions speak louder than words." I appreciate sayings like that. As an old Zen master once said to me, "Don't talk, act!"

What makes people happy is doing, not just wishing. We can spend time complaining or we can spend time changing the world. There is not enough time for both.

Madame Bovary tried unsuccessfully to wish reality away. She spent most of her life dreaming she was someone else, living another life. But her secret life was neither heroic nor successful because it wasn't real. It was just a dream. Dreams are like the wisps of clouds that float over Lake Mahopac on summer days. They're not strong enough to hold us up or strong enough to live in. One day about 2,500 years ago, the great Chinese philosopher Chaung Tzu awoke from a sleep in which he had dreamed he was a butterfly sailing on warm Chinese breezes and tasting the nectar of flowers. Upon awakening and finding himself as he was, he asked an interesting question. "Am I a man dreaming that I'm a butterfly, or am I a butterfly dreaming that I'm a man?"

As a philosopher, I don't know if I'm a butterfly or a human being. As a firefighter and ambulance worker, I do know one thing for sure: the day I arrived at the firehouse, I began to experience things that I had never even dreamed about before. The sound of the siren and the flash of red lights in the darkness gave a surreal quality to the landscape, surpassing the landscape of my dreams. The firefighter's world of fire is the stuff that dreams are made of. They dream about fires past and fires to come.

Dreams are an important and revealing part of human experience. They have given us paintings, stories, poems, operas, and inventions. But just as important is the world of our waking lives. This is the most important dream of all, the dream we call "reality." If we are living the right kind of life, our dreams should be in front of us every time we open our eyes. We can spend our lives wishing we were someplace else. But that cheats us in two ways. We are not where we dream and we are not paying attention to the world around us.

I often start my day with a cup of coffee at the firehouse on my way to work. The pot is on and several others who like to stop by on their way out of town are there too. For example, one of our best truck drivers is Gary Link. He works on the midnight shift for the railroad and hangs out at the firehouse during the day. He wears a cowboy hat and can fix anything that is metal and has moving parts. He is not too much of a dreamer. He always has his feet firmly planted wherever he is. Often, as he and I have our morning coffee at the firehouse, he pours me a cup and smiles as he says, "Doctor Frank, it doesn't get any better than this."

8

Birth, or how to pay attention to new beginnings

"Our birth is but a sleep and a forgetting:
The Soul that rises with us,
our life's Star, Hath had elsewhere its setting,
And cometh from afar"

William Wordsworth

If I live to be a hundred, I will never forget the first time I drove an ambulance, lights and sirens blazing, through the center of town on busy day. I was at home one day shortly after joining the department, when a call came over the monitor. It first came over as a "woman in distress." I raced to my car and sped to the firehouse. A few minutes later, my car glided into the parking lot with its blue light flashing. It was ten o'clock on a Monday morning. The siren was still sounding as the door opened and the ambulance pulled out. Jack Casey was in the driver's seat and I climbed in next to him. Jack is a big fellow and even though he is just in his thirties he has gray hair. He is our main daytime EMT. Jack works as a custodian for the school district. The school district allows him to leave for daytime emergencies. This helps our volunteer department greatly.

Shortly after that, we heard Sergeant Mike Johnson, our police dispatcher. "Carmel Police to all Mahopac Falls ambulance monitors. Woman in labor on W.... Street. You are requested to respond, 10:01."

Dispatchers always end by giving the time. They can report the most unbelievable things, call for the biggest emergency in a person's life, and then conclude with something like "10:01" or "19:20." For some reason that still strikes me as odd. Mike Johnson is the master of this. From his tone you could not tell if the call is going to be the biggest of our lives or just something "routine." I say routine with caution because in our business even the most routine call can turn out deadly. The only time I know Mike to get excited is when he calls for a "1087 at 1131." This is code to the patrol car to pick up Mike's lunch at the local deli. The order is famous: a large sandwich, fries and a diet coke. Why the diet coke we could never figure out.

It was good to have Jack sitting next to me. Jack Casey has delivered a couple of babies over the years.

Jack's hair was not always gray. He was hit on the head by a falling beam in the church on the hill when it caught fire years ago. His hair color changed soon after that.

Jack loves to tell stories and often tells different versions. He can't resist a pun or joke. He has one of those real volunteer firefighter's cars with lots of stickers and more lights than the runway at a major airport.

Jack has been an EMT for 22 years, and he has seen it all— the good, the bad, and the "nervous breakdown" calls. The expression, "nervous breakdown" does not refer to the patients; it is what we do on occasion when we get back to the firehouse.

Although I had been a member of the department a few months, I had not yet driven anything. A rookie is supposed to be a member of the department for a year before he or she is allowed to drive any emergency vehicle. To fully appreciate this story, you must understand that I had never been behind the wheel of any large vehicle in my life. I had spent my life driving such cars as the VW bug and Honda Civic hatchback.

The fire department is usually careful about who they let drive the vehicles. It has driver training and testing, obstacle courses, and a lot of truckers who know how to handle vehicles. They don't want to entrust a $70,000 ambulance to someone who doesn't know what he is doing.

We sat for a minute, Casey behind the wheel and me sitting next to him. Usually there are three or four people in the ambulance when it rolls. But at this point there were only the two of us with no one else in sight. Suddenly the tones went off again and the siren, about 50 feet away, started wailing. Mike Johnson came on again, this time a little more excited.

"Carmel Police to all Mahopac Falls home ambulance monitors, your ambulance is requested on W…. Street for a woman in labor, you are requested to respond forthwith."

The most significant thing in this message was the code word, "forthwith." This is EMS jargon that means, "quit fooling around and get there, people—this is serious!" A "forthwith" call usually means that someone is dying or something extremely serious is happening. Jack looked over at me and bit his lip.

"Have you ever driven a truck before?" he asked.

"Never." I was getting anxious.

Once more, the pagers went off and siren sounded. Again the call came over the airways to respond forthwith. No one else was in sight. It was just Jack and I. The baby was coming and it would take ten or fifteen minutes to call the next department for mutual aid and another ambulance. Could the mother wait that long? Jack looked back at me.

"Never?" he asked again.

I gulped. "Never!!"

"Well," he said as he started to change places with me, "you're gonna learn today!!"

Jack was going to act as the EMT and not the driver. This meant he had to get in the back and get set for the call. He could not drive and do that at the same time. So I was on stage and Jack was coaching me.

I put the ambulance in drive and slowly pulled out. Jack called us out to the sheriff's department dispatcher and told him we were responding.

"19-7-1 to 40 control, responding to an EMS call on W.... Street."

How strange that big rig and big motor felt after all those years of driving cars with motors smaller than a tape recorder. Eventually we turned onto Route 6N by the Baptist church and I started to accelerate. Jack was getting impatient with my slow driving.

"I know you're new at this, but could you do me a favor?"

I knew what he was going to say, but I gave him his set-up line anyway.

"What, Jack?"

He yelled, "Punch it, and let's get there!"

So I "punched it." We found a woman in distress, ready to deliver. Her contractions were a few minutes apart and she was dilated. We picked her up on the stretcher and loaded her into the ambulance.

Jack climbed in the back and I jumped behind the wheel and headed for the hospital. I knew it was just ten minutes away, but could the baby be that patient?

Jack was yelling at me not to get us killed; I was sweating; the siren was wailing, and the woman was moaning. We ran red lights and powered through the busy center of town as fast as we could go. I was flying down the yellow line in the middle of the road hoping that the new arrival could wait until another two or three minutes. As I flew, running lights and dodging parked cars, I listened to the radio. It was Marvin Gaye and Tammy Terrell doing *Ain't no mountain high enough.*

The ambulance powered past cars that had pulled to the side of the road as we raced against time. Jack kept on pumping me as to where we were and what our time frame was. By the time I got on the straightaway to the hospital I was covered with sweat. We accelerated and soon I could see Putnam Hospital in the distance.

When we got to the hospital, the nurses were waiting outside and jumped in the back to help out. Was I happy to see them!

We unloaded our patient and she was rushed inside. We stayed with her for a little bit and finally, glad the baby would be born at the hospital, headed back out to the rig. As we got outside and walked toward the ambulance, I asked Jack if he would mind if I drove it back.

"No thanks," he said, "I'd prefer to get back in one piece."

When we arrived back at the firehouse, we got a phone call from the hospital. The baby had come—a beautiful baby boy. Mother and child were doing well and everything had turned out all right.

The moment of birth is one of the most special and magical moments we humans know. It is moment of pain, courage, and excitement. It is the moment when someone brand new comes into the world and humanity makes a fresh start. When I was in graduate school studying philosophy, I was lucky enough to get to know one of the great philosophers of our century, Hannah Arendt. She theorized that more men than women are preoccupied with death. After he is born, the next big event in a man's life is his death. But women, she wrote, can think in terms of birth, new beginnings, and a fresh start. In her historical studies, she was interested in how something wholly new, like the American Constitution or the French Revolution had come about. Birth, for her, became a metaphor for the intellectual life and the search for renewal. According to her theory, whenever there is a revolution in music or literature, it is a kind of birth; a new movement in philosophy or art can cause a rebirth of that form. This could be said of Mozart and the Beatles. Both brought about changes in the way music is made.

The firefighters and EMS volunteers are just as excited as everyone else when they get a call that a woman is in labor and a baby is on the way. We are trained to keep cool and remember that when everyone else is losing his or her cool it is our job to keep ours.

When the call comes that there is a woman in labor, things often get jumbled. It's one of those special calls. Often in all of the excitement we forget ourselves a little.

Sometimes, in bad weather, people call the ambulance when they would have driven to the hospital themselves if the roads were clear. A few years ago, there was a snowstorm that had the entire county at a standstill. Snow had fallen all day and into the night and so a few us were sleeping at the station. There is an ambulance dorm that sleeps three people and we often stay there in bad weather so we do not have to worry about driving to the station to get a truck out. We had had a very bad chimney fire earlier in the evening, when Walt Swarm and I had almost crashed when the 1972 Mack went into a skid going down a hill toward a car that had spun out at the bottom. Snow continued to fall most of the night, so we spent a lot of time listening to the weather reports and plowing the parking lot so the trucks could get out.

Sometime after midnight, the tones went off again. There was a woman in labor, with contractions three minutes apart, in one of the most mountainous parts of our district. The two EMTs who were on duty went with Tony Luccaro, who was driving the ambulance. We sent along our pickup truck (we call it a brush truck) with the plow attached to clear the road for the ambulance. The snow was falling so hard when they headed out that you couldn't see your hand in front of your face. Two of us stayed back at the main station to monitor the radio.

The chief at that time was an old fashioned gentleman who had rather fixed ideas about how things were to be done. The ambulance was well en route to the scene when we heard his voice over the radio.

"19-1-1 to the Mahopac Falls responding ambulance."

The ambulance signed on and we heard the chief's suggestion.

"On your way to the call you will pass the house of a woman I know. She's a practical nurse. If you stop at her house and wake her up, I'm sure she would come with you. I think a woman having a baby would appreciate another woman in the rig."

We knew this particular woman. She was getting on in years and we were sure she was fast asleep at that time.

Tony got on and said that that wouldn't be needed. He didn't think that shanghaiing citizens at one o'clock in the morning during a major blizzard was a good idea. So the ambulance crew headed to the scene. Everything seemed under control.

When they arrived in the driveway they tried to plow it with the brush truck but the incline was too steep. Then they attempted to get the ambulance up the steep driveway but couldn't make it. At this point, the chief showed up with his four-wheel drive Chevy Blazer. We used the chief's car to get up to the front door. He transported the expectant mother down to the ambulance. They made it to the hospital and she gave birth to a little baby girl a short time afterwards.

The punch line to this story occurred much later at the chief's roast. Whenever a chief goes out of office, we give him a night of fun we call a "roast." It is our final way of saying thank you for all he has done and it is also a chance to get back a few licks. We recount some of the great moments of his reign. We also remind him of those not-so-great moments. When this particular chief was roasted, we recalled that he was very active at trying to recruit new members, even if it involved recruiting citizens after midnight during a blizzard.

In a small-town fire department, many of the members are the sons and daughters of older members. There are people like Walt Swarm, whose families have had three generations that served in the Falls fire department. Many of our members grew up in the firehouse and remember playing on the big rigs when they were as young as three years old.

Every now and then, someone in the department will have a baby and bring it in for all of us to see. Recently one of our members brought in their first baby, a bundle of energy and joy. It was a Friday night and the bar was open. We were all sitting around listening to WHUD playing a *Piano Man* by Billy Joel and sipping beer when the proud parents came in with their newborn. The mother opened the little bundle so we could see the baby with her tiny eyes closed. Walt Swarm and Art Brady smiled as they looked. You could see the joy they took in that baby. They had seen a lot of babies born over the years. They had seen generations of children grow up in the Falls. I cradled her in my arms for a few precious minutes. It didn't last long; everyone wanted to hold her. The old and new were mingling on a Friday night at the Falls firehouse. So much of what the volunteers deal with has to do with the end of things. It warms the heart when once in a while they can be there to help with a beginning.

Hannah Arendt knew that beginnings were special events. Every new beginning is like a birth. Some beginnings, like some births are more dramatic and difficult than others. At the Falls firehouse, we have been reborn, every one of us, into that life that emergency rescuers live. Being there at those moments reminds us in the midst of the worst tragedies that new beginnings can often be found. Every day is a new chance to do it right. Every day is a new chance to say, "I love you" to someone, to take the time to appreciate the beauty of a newly fallen snow, or tell someone how much he or she mean to you. There is always time enough for a new beginning. I sometimes think that is why God made mornings.

9

Separation, or how to successfully navigate the transitions of life

One might compare the journey of the soul to mystical union, by way of pure faith, to the journey of a car on a dark highway...it is by the light of reason that we interpret the signposts and make out the landmarks along our way

Thomas Merton

The years passed quickly after I joined the fire department. That world was so absorbing that I began to pay more attention to my new hobby than the projects I had dealt with for years. It was not enough to have my pocket pager on all day long. I went out and bought a scanner so that I could listen to the police, the neighboring fire departments, and all of the ambulance calls in our county and the surrounding counties. It became a sort of electronic gossip that I could listen in on. There had been a time when I corresponded with philosophers in other countries and regularly talked on the phone with my colleagues from the college. But gradually my contacts with that world became fewer. More and more, I lived for the emergency services. The scanner and pager were next to my bed and I kept them on at night and slept with one ear open.

Eventually, the electronic forest I had raised around me became a wall. Sometimes I thought I should take the pager and throw it out the window, but I didn't. My fascination with the world of fire kept me hypnotized. I was a moth drawn to the flame. I devoted as much time to learning about fires as I had once devoted to the works of Kant and Plato.

The German Philosopher Martin Heidegger wrote from the 1920s until the 1970s. He was another in a long line of philosophers called "Existentialist." This title signifies little because it indicates a group of thinkers who didn't agree on too much. They had very few things in common. They were thinkers who were suspicious of too much thinking. The Existentialists were people of thought who spent a lot of time talking about action. For this reason it is often hard to talk about them. Heidegger had some interesting ideas, including a concept he called "Dasein," a German word that means something like "being there." It can represent the person we could be, our authentic self.

Heidegger felt that some people never live life on their own terms. What did he mean by the word "authentic?" He thought the authentic person was one who was not part of the crowd. This person refused to be a cog in the wheel of business and lived a life that society would not sanction. The authentic person thought about who he was and lived life at his own pace and on his own terms. This does not mean that he joined motorcycle gangs or robbed banks. He lived in the moment and paid attention to the present. It may be possible to be authentic and live a very quiet life. Yet sometimes the road of authenticity takes people away from the life they have known.

Why aren't more of us authentic? The reasons are many and complex. Being authentic requires great character and courage. The consequences of this choice can include the disapproval of our family and friends. We can become outcasts for making unpopular choices. The price to pay is very great. But there is something more. To be authentic often means that we must do things that make us feel uncomfortable. It means to step out on our own into loneliness and fear. It means separating ourselves from our past life and old habits. That is always a frightening move to make.

Step by step, I had begun to separate myself from my old life at the college. There was a time when I spent all of my time in the library studying, or researching, or wandering about the campus. I would visit my friend, Joel, in the English department or Stan, in Sociology and talk about books or campus politics. But now, when class was over, I would spend an hour or two in my office and leave without seeing my old friends. The life of the firefighter and the excitement of the ambulance were very seductive. It called me in the way that drinking calls an alcoholic or gambling calls the addicted gambler. It became my obsession.

There was a time when translating a line of ancient Greek thrilled me. There were years when I studied Chinese writing and texts written in Latin about magic or the Holy Grail. But I no longer visited the library. Now I spent my time reading about pumpers, ladder trucks, and ambulances. I started to take classes that taught me how to handle a hazardous-materials incident and call in a helicopter for a critically injured patient. I would practice putting on my gear and air bottle so I could do it all in less than a minute. I wanted to be the best firefighter in our department.

My free time was now spent at the firehouse, working on the trucks or going on calls. I would sign up for ambulance duty three or four nights a week and go to every fire or rescue that I could. I was spending enough time at the firehouse to get friendly with Walt Swarm and Tommy Stasiak. Whenever the trucks rolled, I wanted to be on board with the wind in my face and my heart racing. More and more, I separated myself from all that I had been before.

One day, the conflict between my two lives came to a head. It was about ten one morning when I was at home typing on my computer and waiting for an important phone call. I had applied for a job teaching at a college in the South. I had done this despite the fact that Mercy College had a wonderful philosophy department and I liked the faculty and the students there. I had published a number of scholarly papers and my friends in other colleges told me I should think about spending a few years at a larger research university. They told me it was time for a change. A job had come up that exactly fit my qualifications and I had sent in my *vita*. I had flown down for an interview and had been told that I was one of the finalists. That day, a phone call would decide my future. The chairman of the philosophy department had told me that there would be a conference call. I had to be there when that phone rang because he needed to decide immediately.

Suddenly, the pager went off. Slow-talking Mike Johnson was on the air.

"Carmel Police to Mahopac Falls fire monitors, report of a structure fire on A…. Road."

There was a moment of hesitation. I knew that phone call was coming. Although my heart was always at Mercy College, I thought I needed to keep on moving to further my career. But I also knew that just a few miles away the lives of my friends would be in danger. Would I wait for the phone call or ride the truck with Tommy Stasiak and Walt? It didn't take long for me to decide what to do.

I turned off the computer, ran to my car, and drove to the firehouse. Swarm already had the attack truck out with its lights flashing and Jack Casey was in the passenger's seat, so I jumped onto the back of the rig with Tony Luccaro. We climbed up onto the hose bed and began to put on our turnout gear. The truck slowly began to roll. Walt caught second gear and the engine whined as the old Mack picked up speed. In a minute, we were flying. By the time we turned the corner, our siren was wailing and we were ready for whatever was to come.

It's a wonderful experience to ride on the back of a fire truck with all of its lights and sirens blazing. There is an indescribable energy to it. A firefighter going to a confirmed working structure fire, riding on the first due engine knows that something exciting is probably going to happen. At college there are never rushes like that. There, every day, there are little victories and little triumphs and we move ahead patiently and with care. But when your life is at stake, everything takes on a different perspective.

When we arrived at the scene, the chief and Stasiak were already there. Smoke was coming out of every window and we could see flames—dark orange flames—rolling in a ball out a back window. Casey and Swarm were getting the water flowing and Tony and I grabbed the nozzle and ran for the front door. We put on our masks and felt the hose stiffen and shake as we got water pressure from the attack truck. We crouched down and felt the door handle from the side. Firefighters never want to stand right in front of a door when they open it. If there is fire behind that door waiting for a breath of air, it will come roaring out like a freight train. We opened the door from the side and black smoke came billowing out. We breathed deep into our masks and bottled air began to blow into our faces as we turned to go inside.

Tony was on the nozzle and I was right behind as we crawled into the black smoke. I saw a flashlight beam over our heads and I knew Stasiak was right behind us, searching for victims. As we crawled forward, we could feel the heat building up and I knew that soon we would see it—the light, the fire, the source of all of that destruction.

We turned a corner and I had to squint because of the heat and brightness. It was like looking into the sun. We opened the nozzle and steam poured over us. Tony inched his way forward into the burning room. The flames rolled over our heads as we reached the source of the fire. We were there to kill it, and it was biting back. Tony turned the nozzle straight up and began to pour water over the ceiling and back down on us. Steam hissed all around us. In the second it took those drops of water to go up to the roof and come back down, they had been heated. The roof was so hot it was cooking all of the droplets of water we were pouring on it. Those droplets went up as water and came back down as steam. The fire was still rolling as we moved towards it. The heat was overwhelming and the smoke was swirling. Tony disappeared in the steam that covered everything.

Later, when we returned outside to report that the fire was under control, I met Stasiak sitting on the back of the attack truck. Swarm was smoking one of his customary cigars and Casey was making some joke about our cowardice. I sat down next to them. Just then Tony Luccaro made a suggestion that startled me.

"You know Doc, this is the year the senior lieutenant moves up to captain and there are going to be a couple of openings for a lieutenant. You've got the time; think about it."

I was shocked. I had only dreamed of doing that, but when Tony—a real firefighter—suggested it, I knew I had a chance. Walt Swarm was quick to add his two cents to the conversation.

"Tony, what, are you kiddin'? The Pa'fessor here, a lieutenant? Don't make me laugh! Pa'fessor, I got a shock for ya, ya can't put out a fire by beatin' it with some book!"

I didn't let that bother me. That's what I would have expected Swarm to say. "Real men" can't pretend they like "pa'fessors." As I rode back to the firehouse on the truck with Tony Luccaro, he encouraged me more.

"Man, if you got the time, go for it. The only thing that ever stopped me from running was the free time."

When I got home, I was soaking wet, my face had soot on it, and I smelled like smoke. There was a message on the answering machine. The job was still a possibility but they wanted to ask me a few more questions. I smiled and erased the message. I never called them back and they never called me back either. They had called and I hadn't been there. I had known that I had to make a decision that day. I walked out into the backyard of my house and sat down at the picnic table. I watched a butterfly land on a tulip. Its orange and black wings were fluttering slowly as it sipped the nectar from the bud. I didn't want to think at that moment. For the first time in years I knew where I was going. The radio was tuned to WHUD and Ann Murray was singing *Snowbird*. The sun felt good on my face. I looked up at the clouds drifting by and felt a great sense of inner peace.

Becoming a professor of philosophy had taken me many years of study and work. I had thought that in a classroom I could be myself. I had thought that it was a life that could make me authentic. In some senses, it did. I loved teaching and I loved talking about the big questions. But there was something about firefighting, the life of action, which was attractive in a different way. Both lives spoke to different parts of myself. They were both languages I enjoyed speaking. Combining thought and action in my two lives satisfied me in many ways. It was one of those moments of realization we have from time to time where all of the pieces seem to fall into place. I had "gotten it." This realization was made clearer to me when I remembered talking to a psychotherapist friend of mine about my love of firefighting. She remembered that I had told her that I, like many people, had experienced some chaos and difficulty in my childhood. She theorized that by going back into the chaos of fire I was returning to something I knew. But more than that, I was now no longer the victim of chaos but was "re-parenting" myself. I was fixing what had been broken. Now I had the power to stop the chaos and the pain and return things to their right path. Fighting fires and going on ambulance calls was doing some healing work in my life. It was working a kind of practical therapy for me.

Martin Heidegger wrote that we are "spit out" or "thrown" into this world. He thought our individual selves are separated from "Being", and have a sense of being lost or homeless. There is a sense or impulse inside of us that seeks home. It is this sense of homesickness that guides us through this world. It is through our choices every day that we try to remake that bond that we often feel is so lacking in our lives. We are separate from Being, the great source, what Lao Tzu would call the Tao, or the Great Mother, which nourishes all things. We are here to find our way home. Like fire, we are here to find our own way. In my garden, at that moment, I realized I was on the right path.

All of us come to junctures in our lives where it is hard to see the right path. These moments of transition will define all that comes after them. That is the time to quiet our minds and listen to our heart. It is my belief that our heart never lies, ever.

I kept up my efforts at the firehouse through the summer and fall, and that September I was elected a lieutenant in the Mahopac Falls Volunteer Fire Department.

10

Difference, or what we should really look for in a person

We can most safely achieve universal tolerance when we respect that which is characteristic in the individual and in nations, clinging, though to the conviction that the truly meritorious is unique by belonging to all mankind.

Johann Wolfgang Von Goethe

I remember the first time I heard Martin Luther King's "I Have a Dream" speech. In his dream, all children had a chance in life. In his vision, people could live with each other in peace and without fear. He imagined a society in which we would accept each other as we are. He wanted us to judge each other not by the color of our skin but by the quality of our character.

Everybody wants to be accepted. The Falls firefighters are peculiar about that. In some ways they will accept anybody. If a person puts in an application, knows his left foot from his right, and can climb a ladder, he will become a member. This is not as difficult as getting a Ph.D. from one of the elite graduate schools in German philosophy. It is easy to join most local volunteer fire departments. However, to be accepted, really accepted, takes time and effort.

Although it is not too difficult to join, we have some members who wish we were more selective. Some of the tough old-timers have voted against almost every new member. They are very democratic and do not discriminate. They are equal-opportunity nay-sayers. Breaking into this small society takes some effort. The process of becoming a real member takes years. It is something that takes time and commitment.

Today, there are several female firefighters in the Falls, but that wasn't always the case. Patty O'Keefe was the first female member and when she applied there was almost a riot. It was in the 1980's when no woman had ever attended a drill. But Patty wanted to join. She wanted to ride the ambulance.

Patty was the head nurse at the Emergency Room at Putnam hospital. She is smart, medically knowledgeable, and tough. But there were other factors that some of the old-timers hadn't missed. Patty is a young, attractive woman. She is petite, has long blond hair, and a constant smile. She doesn't look like your "typical" firefighter and the members weren't so sure that this would work out. Up until that time, the firehouse had always been a men's club. It was a place members could relax and be themselves. They could shoot a game of pool, take off their shoes, put their feet up, and wear their old clothes. In short, it was a place where they could feel as comfortable as if they were in their own home. Someone once called the firehouse "the poor man's country club." What if suddenly a beautiful young woman could walk in anytime she wanted to? The "boys" weren't so sure this was a good idea.

The night her name was presented for membership on the meeting room floor, she was not allowed to be present. This was according to the rule for all new members. As you might imagine, there was a big argument on the floor. Tempers flared, fingers were pointed, and some angry words were spoken. Some people said a woman would ruin the department. Others wondered why it would be a bad thing. Some people said that a firefighter had to be a man because a woman did not have the strength to do the job. Other people argued that a woman could handle ambulance calls.

When it came time for the ballots, she didn't have the votes to get in. But Patty was tough, and she applied again the next month. Again, there was a big fight on the floor and the situation almost got out of hand. Tony Luccaro, champion of modern causes at the Falls firehouse, was butting heads with some of the most influential of the old-timers. It was a difficult and long night. When it was all over and the votes were in, Patty had made it. She was the first woman to become an official member of the Mahopac Falls Volunteer Fire Department.

Before that, women had been associated with the department for half a century. The Ladies Auxiliary did a lot for the old-time firefighters. Most of the members of the auxiliary were the wives of firefighters, but there were always a few who weren't. The ladies would raise money for the department and make food when the firefighters were out all night at a fire. When firefighters have been out for five or six hours in sub-zero temperatures, they appreciate coming back to the station and finding hot soup and sandwiches. In the years before the electric pagers and the siren, there used to be a phone tree. The police would call several women in the Falls, and they in turn would call the firefighters. Walt Swarm's wife made those calls for years, and we recently attended the funeral for another of the original callers. But no woman had ever been an official "active member" until Patty joined.

As you might guess, Patty wasn't that popular at first. The firefighters were not going to make it easy for Patty, either. They made her climb ladders, run along roofs, and hold a hose with two hundred pounds of pressure coming out of the nozzle. She was married to Ritchie, who is a police officer in town and a Mahopac firefighter. I always laugh about the rivalry between the two departments when I think of Patty and Ritchie, who have sometimes carried out the battle in their house in the center of town.

Eventually, Patty became an ambulance lieutenant and later became ambulance captain. She was a good and no-nonsense captain who raised the level of our medical training. Ten years later, there are more than a dozen women in the department. They occupy key roles in the firehouse and are very involved in every aspect of our operation. One of my favorite firefighters is Camille Lapine. Camille has gone even further than Patty. Though she is a nurse and an EMT instructor, Camille considers herself foremost a firefighter. She owns a Dalmatian named "Backdraft" and always wears firehouse logos wherever she goes. So when Camille arrives at a fire and they try to push her towards the ambulance she resists. Camille has been an officer at the Falls and has given us the best of her heart. She is part of Patty's legacy.

America has had a race problem for a long time. People are often judged more by what they are then who they are. There is a story I heard when I first joined the Falls that gave me some hope. It is the story of a man named Bill Andrews.

Bill Andrews was the head of the only African American family in Mahopac Falls in the 1940s. Like me, Bill got a notion in his head that he wanted to join the Mahopac Falls Volunteer Fire Department. He put in his application and waited to hear the results of the vote. In those days, the firefighters were a little more selective about who got in than they are today. When it came time to vote, they used a box of marbles. Most of the marbles were white, but three were black. Each firefighter would walk up to the table, pick out a marble, and drop it in the box. If the new applicant got three black marbles he was "blackballed."

You might have thought that Bill Andrews would be the perfect candidate to be blackballed, but Bill had been in town a while and some of the people at the Falls knew and liked him. He was a person who worked hard and was always there to lend a hand in time of need. Bill didn't get one black ball and was admitted to the department.

Bill made himself a fixture at the Falls for more than thirty years. When it came time to rewrite the by-laws and establish standard operating procedures for fires, Bill was put in charge and most of what he wrote still holds today. When people mention Bill's name it's with great admiration.

In the late 1960's, a wave of racial unrest spread over the nation. There were riots, sit-ins, and burned cities. There was a strong anger on the part of a lot of people. The Mahopac Falls Volunteer Fire Department was not immune to the turbulence. A civil rights organization thought that fire departments had discriminated against African Americans. They decided to start a fact-finding mission to see how many blacks were members of fire departments, paid and volunteer, all across America. They mailed a questionnaire to every fire department in the country.

One day a letter arrived at the Falls fire department asking how many members of color there were, whether there were any patterns of discrimination, and what the minority population of the town was.

At the time of the survey there were two African American families in the Falls. The president of our department wrote back proudly to that civil rights organization that fifty percent of the African American families in town were represented in our department.

I am not saying there have never been unkind words or some cruel remarks said in the firehouse. Sometimes things can be a little heated down at the coffee pot. There have been times when I have heard some rather unenlightened views expressed down there. Nevertheless, firefighting is something that is hard to fake. So, in time, your heart is revealed more clearly than in many other professions. It has a way of stripping you down to what you are essentially. It is a way for us to see clearly. If someone can stand beside you when the walls are burning and your helmets are melting, you learn to respect that person no matter who they are. When the temperature gets hot enough, it will not matter what the gender, color, or religion of the firefighter watching your back.

Bill Andrews eventually became ill. Near the end, they used to transport him to his doctors and back and forth from the hospital in the Falls ambulance. Bill is no longer with us, but what he was will always be a part of our family.

Religion has never been a big issue at the department. I think that has something to do with the unique history of our town. In the old days, when the town was a resort with big hotels on the lake, a large number of Jewish people from New York City were summer residents. Because of the large Jewish population, anti-Semitism was never as strong here as it was in some other places I've visited. I think if you know enough people of a given group it is more difficult to discriminate against them. Knowing a person with all of their good and bad points takes the wind out of any easy stereotypes. Our town also has every Christian denomination you can think of, a few Muslim families, and a number of Buddhists and Hindus.

I think the real religious views of Mahopac residents can be seen in the bingo schedule. You can start on Monday night at Temple Beth Shalom and play bingo at a different house of worship every night of the week. The bingo fanatics are very liberal when it comes to where they play.

One autumn day a group of firefighters went to the funeral of one of our twenty-year members who had died and was being laid to rest in the cemetery of the Baptist church across the street. We put on our dress uniforms and walked over to the little ceremony. Because it was during the week, only about ten of us were able to show up.

Although the cemetery is behind the Baptist Church, anyone can buy a plot and be buried there. The twenty-year member we were there to honor had been Jewish. The rabbi was there behind the Baptist Church. He was joined by ten firefighters. Almost all of us there attended a different house of worship. There was something heartwarming about that. It occurred to me one day, after I had been in for about two years, that I didn't know the religion of any of the other firefighters. I had seen some of them in Saint John's Catholic Church, where I go, but for most of the members I can't say if they are church going or not.

At the funeral, I mentioned to Tommy Stasiak that I couldn't remember a single conversation about religion in all the time I had been at the firehouse.

He smiled. "I know. Isn't it great?"

Many of us have different beliefs but we don't let them in the door at the firehouse. I was thinking about that at the cemetery, when Charlie Locke and Tommy Stasiak started talking about buying the plots where they would be buried. Stasiak grinned.

"I should get myself a plot here."

Charlie looked around at the orange maples and little brook. "Yeah, it would be nice to be close to the firehouse."

Tommy liked the idea. "You know, you could hear the siren from here."

Soon we were back across the street at the firehouse by the coffee pot. The radio was tuned to WHUD playing the Wee Five's *You Were On My Mind*.

At that instant it occurred to me what Tommy Stasiak's religion really was. Although Tommy is a Catholic, he is also a firefighter. Just as he worships in church every Sunday, he also gives himself to the fire department. And he wanted to be buried close to the place that was so much in his heart.

There is a wide range of political beliefs at the firehouse, too. We don't talk politics very often, but when we do, there are a variety of opinions. Some people, like Walt Swarm, are old-time conservatives. We have members who landed on the beach on D-Day and profess the views you might expect of old-time VFW members. Tony Luccaro is one of our resident liberals. Tony and Walt oftentimes exchange their political theories in the most entertaining way. These conversations are intense and we always have some interesting debates. There is no single fire department opinion on anything. When we have elections, we have more arguments among ourselves than you would believe.

At our monthly meetings, Walt Swarm is ready to jump on anybody who stands up and doesn't know what they are talking about. When we argue, our discussions can get very heated and sometimes cross that line into some personal anger. Recently we had a big battle about selling one of our old trucks. We fought about that for months, and people are still mad. But that is okay. Expressing our views honestly is one of the values that keep the fire service going.

Some clubs are harder to get into than others. The Ph.D. club is rather exclusive, and that is what makes the title "Doctor" worth something at colleges. Being accepted into the Falls fire department took just as much work as getting my Ph.D.. It doesn't matter if you are black, female, or Muslim. The Falls firefighters don't pay too much attention to little details like that. They are too enlightened to be fooled that easily.

It is easy and lazy to judge a person by what they are rather than who they are. To say that someone cannot do something because of his or her gender, race, or religion demeans all of us. We are connected in ways that are subtle and complex. I remember talking to a professor of physics one day who explained to me that each person is made up of atoms and atoms are also in the air between us. So in a sense, each of us is touching and impinging on the other all of the time in ways we may not be able to measure. What happens to you is what happens to me. How I treat you will impact the world that I live in. No one is above this and no one should forget this. We are all part of the same journey.

Martin Luther King didn't live to see his dream fulfilled. Still, that dream is the American Dream. I, too, would like to judge each person by what he does and not by what I think he should be. I, too, dream of a world in which people give other people the same chance that they want for themselves. Dreams are funny sometimes. Sometimes you can catch one from somebody else, like you would catch a cold. The dream of accepting the new has always been the American Dream. That's how this country was born and how it grew. It was Jefferson's dream, and it was King's dream. They are no longer here to sustain that dream. It's our dream now.

11

Courage, or how to trust your heart at the right moment

*It is curious—curious that physical courage should be
so common in the world, and moral courage so rare*

Mark Twain

"Move it, pa'fessor!" Walt Swarm yelled as he started up the fire truck.

"We got a house on fire!" It was two-thirty in the morning on a warm May night and the firehouse was alive with scrambling bodies. I ran toward the attack truck with my gear bag and helmet and jumped into the passenger seat. Old Walt was chewing on his cigar as usual and wearing his Mack Truck baseball cap. He looked over at me. "What are ya waitin' for? Better get dressed pa'fessor. Sounds like we got a cooker!"

I was getting dressed as fast as I could, which was way too slow for Walt. He kept rolling his hand with that signal that means, "get going!" Other cars with flashing blue lights pulled into the parking lot as two more fire trucks pulled out onto the blacktop. I looked behind me and saw that we had three firefighters in the jump seat behind me. Walt was anxious to get going so I told him, "We got a full crew. Let's roll!"

He looked at me with a look of disgust that it has taken him sixty years to perfect. "I got eyes, pa'fessor. Call us out!"

I picked up the microphone as the truck began to roll. "Mahopac Falls 19-2-3 to Forty Control." I waited a minute for them to acknowledge.

"Forty Control is on, 19-2-3. Go ahead with your message."

I pressed the button on the microphone and tried to talk over the blaring siren. "Mahopac Falls Attack truck 2-3. One rescue truck and one tanker are responding at this time to a structure fire on B.... Drive."

I looked into the rearview mirror and saw the other trucks with their lights and sirens going as they followed us into the night. Walt pointed to the horizon. There it was, the dragon. The sky was orange, and black smoke was billowing up. I took a deep breath as I finished buttoning my coat and put on my lieutenant's helmet. I was already starting to sweat. Suddenly our tones went off again on the radio.

"Carmel Police to all Mahopac Falls Fire Monitors. All available manpower is needed for a fully involved working structure fire on B.... Drive. Occupants believed trapped inside."

We were going to need a good deal of courage that night. This was especially interesting for me, as I had been thinking all day about what courage is. In my Introduction to Philosophy class at Mercy College, we had been reading the Ethics of Aristotle. Aristotle was the student of Plato. Plato had talked about the "Forms" or "Ideas," which for him meant the fixed definitions of things. For example in one of Plato's dialogues, someone asks,

"What is Justice?" as if Justice was the same for everyone. Then someone else asks, "What is Goodness?" as if there were only one answer to that question. Although he wasn't as poetic as his teacher, Aristotle was subtler. When Aristotle spoke about ideas like truth, justice or goodness, he saw them less abstractly and less simplistically. For him, different places and different times gave us different virtues. What is good for one person in one age may not be good for another person at another time.

This is true of all virtues, and courage is no exception. First, it's a virtue that differs from person to person and from place to place. What may be very courageous for one person may not be courageous at all for another. My firefighting friend Tommy Stasiak, who works as a corrections officer, is used to dealing with threatening situations while many professors at Mercy College are not. One of my friends, Howard, is a gentle professor of English Literature whose day is filled with books and notes. So responding to a physical assault takes more courage from Howard than from Tommy, who has been trained to deal with such situations. What Aristotle told us is that courage for a soldier in war is different from that of a person who has to struggle every day with a long, debilitating illness. Courage is a mean between two extremes. Too much courage is a bad thing; it can make us foolhardy and reckless, so that we hurt both others and ourselves. Too much courage can be as bad as no courage at all. Too little courage means that we are cowardly and passive—another undesirable quality. It means that fear rules our lives and that we lack the control we need. Each of us must relate our ethical values to our own backgrounds and find our own middle ground, our own rhythm.

Walt was chomping on his cigar as he pulled the air horn to let the chief know we were only a mile away. He talked to me without taking his eyes off the road.

"Pa'fessor, we're gonna be the first truck in, so you and those guys in the back are gonna be the first due inside. You better take a look back there and see who ya got."

I turned and looked through the glass at the three members in the back. The team was a good one. Tommy Stasiak was already dressed, cursing in a way that only seasoned corrections officers can do. In the second seat was Camille Lapine who was the newest addition to our crew. The third man was Tony Luccaro.

When we made the turn onto B.... Drive, we could smell the smoke. In small rural America there are not fire hydrants everywhere a firefighter needs them; that's why fire trucks carry so much hose on the back. The hose is already connected so it can be taken off even before the truck stops. When we first turned off the main road onto B.... Drive, the truck paused for a minute. Camille got out and took one of the big hoses off the back of the truck and wrapped it around a tree. She then signaled the truck to go forward. As the truck went on, the hose came out of the back of the truck in a straight line. It was through this hose that water would later be sent when the big tanker hooked up to it.

As we approached the scene, we saw the fire burning, licking red and orange into the night sky. It was already through the roof. Even though it was almost 2:45 in the morning, all of the neighbors were out on their lawns watching the fire that was now blazing through the roof and out the picture window of the raised ranch. Some of them were yelling and crowding around the trucks though the police were trying to keep them a safe distance away from us.

When I got out of the truck, I already had on all of my equipment. I strapped on an air bottle on the way to the front door. As I walked, I made a last-minute check of the buttons on my coat and made sure I would have everything I needed if the situation got out of hand. Inside a fire, a firefighter must protect every part of his or her anatomy. If there is one opening, the heat will come through and burn you severely. Even though everyone around us is in a panic, we must have the presence of mind to pay attention to the little details. If they are looked after, these little details can save our lives. Even though we are distracted and everyone is vying for our attention, we need to be careful about what we are doing. These moments in the midst of a major fire really test a firefighter's attention and focus. I like to call them "Zen" moments.

With the hose lines stretched from the trucks, a firefighter was breaking down the front door with an axe. The fire was so hot I had to squint. Now that I was only a few feet away from it, I could feel the power of the fire. In just a few minutes we would be through that door and begin our dance with brother fire.

The chief was at the front of the house when we arrived. He turned to me as the door was being axed open. He looked more excited than usual.

"Lieutenant, we have a problem here. The people across the street said there are two people still inside and we've got to go in there and get them out."

The fire was so hot it was hard to believe that anyone inside might still be alive, but we had to try, no matter what the odds were. I looked over at the driveway and saw a car parked. Yes, it looked like somebody might be home. I hoped we were wrong.

The axe smashed through the front door and we could see the brightness of the fire right in front of us. We all took a step back. I felt my pulse racing. We were going to have to do an interior attack and a search-and-rescue at the same time. It was going to be tricky.

I ran back to the big attack truck and asked for some help to pull a line out of the hose bed in the back. The hose came out and we dragged it up to the front door. If we were to have any chance at all, we were going to need plenty of water to cool this fire down. Back at the truck, some of the men and women of the Mahopac Falls Volunteer Fire Department were attaching the lines to the truck and grabbing axes and other tools. We stretched the lines up to the front door and sent another stream of water in through the broken picture window. The ambulance, which comes with us to all major fires, went by with its lights and sirens going. I turned to Tommy Stasiak.

"Who's in the ambulance?"

He was too busy to give a long answer. "One of our guys got burned already, the window blew out and got him."

We were ready to go in and see what we could do. The job of the lieutenant is to go in with the hose line and make sure everything is okay. I turned on my air, put on my mask and took a deep breath. The fire seemed as bright as the sun. I whispered a little prayer and made the sign of the cross as I got low and crept inside. Most firefighters I know are either religious or superstitious. They have all of their lucky charms that they hope will keep them from the fire. It is not enough to be a good firefighter; you have to be lucky as well.

About fifteen feet inside the front door, our attack was stalled. The roof, the walls and the floor were ablaze. The fire was rolling and licking just a foot ahead of us. I yelled to Tommy Stasiak to see if we could go any faster, and he just shook his head. The fire was over us in the attic and every time we pushed it one way with the hose, it whipped around and reappeared somewhere else. When there is fire in only one part of a house, it can be pushed in one direction and attacked more easily. But when it's everywhere, there's no one place to direct it and no real way to control it. Finally, after about fifteen minutes, we got through the flames into a hallway. There was a door in front of us. I told the firefighters to stand back as I felt the door from the side. It was so hot that I could feel it right through my gloves. I smashed it open with the pry bar as we all got low and out of the way. Out raged the fire, almost rolling over our heads. Tony was on the nozzle now and kept spraying the ceiling.

Everything around us was on fire and my facemask was starting to feel hot. We were trying our best to put out the inferno but it was holding us back and throwing balls of fire at us that were bigger than the trucks. Suddenly, the unthinkable happened. The fog stream that was coming out of the nozzle, which was holding the heat and flames just a few feet in front of us, started to shrink. We were losing water pressure; we were losing our shield. It was the only thing that stood between the fire and us. Tony and Camille had run out of air and were outside changing air bottles. Just a minute before, two new members had joined Tommy Stasiak and me.

Stasiak was pointing at my portable radio as he yelled in a muffled voice from inside his mask, "Brother, you better get on that thing and tell them we need water, and not next week!"

I yelled for water through the radio microphone on my collar. A voice on the other end, which I recognized as Walt Swarm's, answered me.

"Keep your shirt on pa'fessor! It's on the way. We were just switching trucks!"

Suddenly the fog stream grew and cooled the air in front of us. Stasiak gave me a thumbs up and we crawled forward. Every inch had to be taken from the fire.

Then I heard a sound that no firefighter likes hearing inside a fire: a rattling that meant the alarm was going off in my mask. This told me that my air was low and I should get out of the fire and get another bottle. I told Tommy and the two others I was going out for another bottle, and Tommy assured me that they had things under control.

"Don't worry about us pal; we're big boys!"

As I got outside, I met Tony and Camille heading back in with fresh bottles of air. They were exhausted but ready to go back on the attack. I pulled off my mask in the cool night air and felt the sweat running down my face. I took a deep breath and walked over to the rescue truck. All of the spare bottles were lined up. One of the rookies helped me take off the old bottle and put a new one in the harness. (To save time, we don't take the harnesses off our backs. We just have someone turn off the old bottle, pull it out, put in a fresh one and turn it on.) In a minute we were ready.

I got my helmet back on, put on my mask, and headed back inside. I saw someone coming out to change bottles. It was Stasiak. I always like talking to Tommy. I couldn't resist asking him a question.

"Hot enough for ya in there?"

At that point, he was in no mood for jokes. "We are takin' a beatin' in there, brother!"

I headed back inside. In the hallway, Tony was on the head of the nozzle and another firefighter was breaking into the last bedroom, hoping desperately to find someone in there. Tony felt the door and yelled out, "Stand back! We got some fire behind this door!"

Tony and the hose team got out of the way and someone forced the door. It opened in a burst of light and heat. The hose team advanced and I took the nozzle as Tony and the rest of the team cleared debris out of our way. A hose line was trained on the roof from outside and water was starting to stream down all over us. We were soaked, our coats were heavy with cold water, and we were exhausted. Our search had turned up nothing.

Later, after almost an hour of fighting the fire and going through two and a half air bottles, I was standing on the lawn of what had once been a house. The walls were blackened and there were pools of dark water everywhere. Now it was only a charred, blackening ruin, collapsing. Everywhere was the smell of burned wood and plastic. Beams and pipes were twisted and bent. It was a strange and foreign landscape that told the story of the fire's journey.

It was four o'clock in the morning and our work for that night was only beginning. We had salvage and overhauling work to do to make sure we had extinguished all of the fire so it wouldn't rekindle and have us back fighting it again the next day. It had been a tough fire for our little department. Even though we fight a few fires like this each year, it is still a shock when one happens. Two of our fire-fighters were hospitalized, one with neck burns and another with smoke inhalation. Another firefighter was hurt later that night when a large heating duct in the ceiling fell in and landed on top of him. Stasiak got him outside and joked that the guy was OK because it hit him where he didn't have much feeling—his head.

Another officer came over to us. He looked exhausted.

"I just talked to the chief. The family was not inside; they were out for the night. So we have no victims as of now."

Tommy and the others were spent. We had changed our normal plan of initial attack to try to rescue whoever was inside that building. Every firefighter I know wants to perform a rescue at least once in his or her career. When Tommy found out that there was nobody inside, he felt an emotional letdown. All that effort was for nothing.

A little while later, the sun came up. Hoses covered the place like a colony of anacondas, and all of our equipment was dirty and wet. We couldn't leave the scene like that. Every piece of equipment had to be "back in service" so that it was ready for the next "big one." You never know, you *never* know when the next fire will happen. It could break out in the next five minutes.

We picked up our hose, took our tools, and began to put the trucks back together at the scene. Inside the house, firefighters were still spraying the ruins and looking for "hot spots." Our faces were black with smoke, our coats were soaking wet, and we were exhausted from being inside. Every muscle in my body ached. I had spent hours crouched down in an unnatural position. My knees were hurting from all of the crawling around I had done. I had forced doors open and pushed any furniture that got in our way. I had dragged the heavy hose with us everywhere we went. I was beat.

We weren't finished until close to seven o'clock, and then we went to our paying jobs. That's what volunteer firefighters do all over America every night. Some of our members who are paid firefighters in New York City would be back riding their trucks and putting out fires on the roofs of warehouses. Tony would go do what he calls the "Lord's work"—working with people with disabilities. Tommy Stasiak would stick a cigar in his mouth, pick up his nightstick and head off to the jail where he worked. Others would be out delivering mail or driving trucks. I had to go to work, too, that morning. I was teaching an ethics course at Mercy College. I was going to talk about Aristotle's concept of courage. I didn't need to read Aristotle that morning to remind myself about courage. I only needed to remember Tony, Camille, and Tommy crawling on their bellies into the lair of the dragon and getting eye-to-eye with the Red Devil.

We went back to the firehouse where the ladies auxiliary had prepared us a breakfast of ham and eggs with a lot of coffee and orange juice. I took my shower, put on my suit and tie, and drove to the college. As I rode in my car past the rolling hills of the Hudson River Valley, I meditated and listened to the oldies on my car radio. It was the Cascades singing *Rhythm of the Rain.*

In no time at all I was in the college parking lot. Mercy College is located on the banks of the beautiful Hudson River. It is full of trees and flowers that are reborn every spring. As I walked to my classroom, I stopped for a moment in front of a magnolia tree in full bloom. The flowers were pink and waved like a silken robe against the blue sky. The tree had been blooming for a week, but somehow that morning it seemed special. That's how being in the heart of a fire can affect the way you look at the world.

I went into the class and we started to read the text. Yes, Aristotle knew a few truths after all. He knew that courage isn't something we talk about; it exists in the things we do. For Aristotle, courage was one of the practical values that we must practice as often as we can. It is a habit that grows slowly and carefully. It will not appear in an instant out of nowhere. It is the fruit that must ripen after a lifetime of work and care.

Courage is a slippery thing. We can't always be sure that it will be there when we need it. I thought about the way Aristotle described courage as being a golden mean between the two extremes of fear and foolhardiness. Neither is good for firefighters. They need courage in their hearts and clarity in their minds to do their job right. It has to be just right, or it will be all wrong.

Philosophy takes courage too. Socrates, the teacher of Plato, who in turn became Aristotle's teacher, once said, "The unexamined life is not worth living." It takes courage to really examine ourselves. It takes heart to ask if there is a better way of living. It takes nerve to change. I think a lot of us would love to be more courageous but instead of trusting our hearts and our feelings, we get too involved in all of the "what ifs" that can get in the way. I think if we listen to our hearts more clearly we almost always know the right path, the courageous path.

Courage is a rare and precious commodity in this world. When it appears, we should honor it, for it is as rare and precious as that magnolia that shows its pink silken glory only for a short time and is gone for another year.

12

Giving, or looking at gifts in a different light

The manner of the giving is worth more than the gift

Pierre Corneille

It was Christmas Eve. It got cold in the middle of the afternoon, and the light turned that unusual shade of yellowish-blue that it has only for a short period in winter. My next-door neighbor, Denis, is an artist and he points out those kinds of things to me. He notices such colors and subtle textures that most people don't look for. Once he had me look at the gray winter sky and asked me how many shades of gray I saw. After just a minute I answered quickly.

"Twelve."

He smiled. He told me I was not looking hard enough or long enough. In time I could pick out many more shades of color. Perhaps that's the way it is with all looking. We look but we don't see. We put our eyes on things but our mind is someplace else. We are inattentively attentive. When a great Zen master was once asked what is important in life he roared, "Attention! Attention! Attention!" Wherever you are, be fully there. Don't have your body in one place and your mind in another. Wherever you are, pay attention, even if it is to the subtle shades of gray.

It had been raining and sleeting on and off for most of the day, and by nightfall the temperatures plunged. All of the Christmas lights were lit on my block and it seemed every radio station was playing carols. The traffic was snarled on Main Street all day long, as everybody hurried out to get that one last little gift that they had forgotten to buy for that favorite nephew. It was the usual thing that happens around here that time of year.

I, myself, was not in too festive a mood that night. I had one of those flu bugs that had just knocked me out. I was aching all over and I was dead on my feet. I had eaten a bowl of chicken soup and was in bed watching television. I wanted to see the version of Charles Dickens's *Christmas Carol* that they always broadcast late at night. There are a couple of film versions of this story, but as far as I'm concerned, there's only one great one.

When you belong to an Emergency Services Department that relies on volunteers, holidays look very different. There is no safe time. There is no moment that is guaranteed unless you decide to turn off the pager and consciously unplug yourself from the grid. There is no season that is sacred from fire or injury. Someone once asked me why I didn't just shut the pager off on Christmas Eve or Thanksgiving. I told them that we have had a very big fire on Thanksgiving for five years in a row. Don't ask me why. Maybe it is the fact that fireplaces have not been used or that old stoves are on all day. But sure enough, around dinnertime every year, the call comes in that one of our neighbor's houses is on fire and we are needed. It is hard to explain the pleasure there is in being the reliable guard dog; there is a certain satisfaction in being there when someone needs us. But it can be difficult for many people to live with this. This is why about half the people that join the fire department are gone a few months later. One day a member's husband or wife says, "turn that damn pager off!" Somehow it never gets turned back on and they go back to that quiet regular life that they lived before the fire department intruded. I meet them later and they ask how it is going, but I often can see they are glad they've left.

Earlier that Christmas Eve I had gotten a call from Tommy Stasiak at the firehouse. All the officers were out of the district at one affair or another except for me. I informed Tommy that, short of a nuclear meltdown, I wasn't getting out of bed. I just couldn't get up.

I had wished Tommy a happy holiday, hung up the phone, and sank into my old bed with its flannel sheets and piles of quilts. I was still cold. It was Christmas Eve in the Falls.

Around 6 o'clock the pager went off. There had been a bad car accident on Route 6N where it winds along the south shore of Lake Mahopac. The rain had frozen into ice and a multiple car accident was testing the resources of our neighboring department, Mahopac. Although the Mahopac Fire Department and Mahopac Falls Fire Department have been rivals for more than half a century, we help each other out along our shared border. I heard our big police dispatcher, Sergeant Mike Johnson on the air. I thought how different the holidays are for police, firefighters and EMS workers compared to other people.

Mahopac needed our fire police. The fire police are members of a volunteer fire department whose main function is to direct traffic, put up flares, and help control the scene. This is needed when we are operating at a scene and need to protect our members from traffic. The whole road had been closed from the center of town all the way down to the street that I live on. A short time later, I heard Mahopac Falls on the air.

"40 Control, this is Mahopac Falls responding to a motor vehicle accident on mutual aid to Mahopac."

Apparently, our friends at the Mahopac fire department were also a little short-handed that night. Soon the pager was filled with communications from the accident scene and it sounded like they had their hands full.

About half an hour later, our tones went off again. There was a medical emergency in the eastern section of our district. They needed an ambulance. I was feeling guilty and tried to sit up a little. I got light-headed and sank back down, feeling pain and frustration, knowing that I could not go.

The call started to sound serious when one of the EMTs on the scene called for the ambulance "forthwith." I could tell by the rising tone of his voice that things weren't going smoothly. About two minutes went by, and then I heard our second ambulance responding to the scene. I recognized Tony Luccaro's voice on the air.

"40 Control, this is Mahopac Falls EMS 19-7-2 responding to a call forthwith on W…. Road."

I was woozy but awake enough to figure out that with the fire police on the west side of the district and a lot of the EMS personnel on the east side of the district, the resources of our department were stretched quite thin for Christmas Eve. That's what it is like to be a volunteer in the fire department. You don't volunteer when it is convenient for you. You don't volunteer when the weather suits you. You volunteer because it is needed. Need knows no holidays and no time of day. When there is a need, the volunteers want to be there.

I rolled over and tried to get back to sleep. About ten minutes later the tones went off again. It was turning into some night! It was Sergeant Mike Johnson again.

"Carmel Police to all Mahopac Falls home ambulance monitors. Your ambulance is requested at R.... Lane, for a male subject who has fallen with a possible broken knee. Time of first notification—19:21."

Suddenly, I was fully awake. It was taking too long for our other ambulance to sign on. 19-7-2 was now en route to Putnam Hospital and could not help them. Mahopac and the fire police were still working at the car accident, and Putnam Valley, the department on our western border, was out at the time as well.

I was getting anxious. The police hit the tones again for more manpower and then a third time. I couldn't stand it. I jumped out of bed, grabbed my portable radio, and called the ambulance. I told them to respond to the scene, that I was on my way, and would meet them there.

I pulled my clothes on over my pajamas and stumbled downstairs. I staggered out into the freezing cold, started my car, plugged in the flashing blue light and took off for the scene. The roads were almost empty and I could make good time. I would be there just after the ambulance. They called in that they were "Off on location." (fire department jargon for "on the scene"!) I told them that I was about a minute away.

Camille Lapine, who was driving the ambulance, let herself get a little informal on a Christmas Eve and radioed back, "We hear ya, Doc."

As I approached the scene, I saw the red lights flashing in the distance. I drove up and parked my car so it would not block the ambulance. I raced inside and found a 19-year-old boy, whose knee had popped out, lying on the living room floor with a house full of relatives around. I think some of them were wondering why I was wearing a pajama top under my coat at 7:30 in the evening, but they were too polite to ask. There was even a woman, whom I took to be his grandmother, giving us advice on how to take special care of her number-one grandson.

"Be careful with his leg!" she cautioned us. "Make sure you don't drop him!" she warned as we picked up the stretcher.

We got the splints out of the ambulance, immobilized his leg, and then had to move half the furniture and Christmas gifts to get the stretcher to the front door. We took his vital signs, looked at the knee and leg, and headed out. We carried him out the door and walked down a slippery, ice-caked driveway, trying not to drop him and injure the other knee. The youngster was smiling, although he had winced with pain when I'd felt the area he said was hurting. He was a good-sized boy with black hair and brown eyes. He was taking it like a trooper and he was going to be okay.

We got aboard the ambulance and then someone showed up to drive my car back to the firehouse. Camille started to drive to Putnam Hospital Center. The roads were icy. There were Christmas decorations everywhere.

As we went through the center of town we passed our other ambulance heading back to the station. Tony Luccaro, the EMT on the first rig, radioed us and told us they had left some of their equipment at the hospital and asked if we could pick it up for them. From the items Tony had mentioned, I could tell it had been a hard call for them to make on Christmas Eve. The objects he was talking about were the tools used for CPR. This meant that whoever had been lying in the back of that ambulance had had no heartbeat, no pulse, and no blood running through his or her veins. It meant that things had probably not gone that well. When I heard that they wanted a bag valve mask, I knew that that meant a spirit who had resided for a while in Mahopac Falls was probably bound for another realm on this winter night.

We made it to Putnam Hospital, dropped off our patient, picked up our supplies, and headed back to the barn. I sat in the front seat with Camille. We had the radio tuned to WHUD and Karen Carpenter was singing *I'll be home for Christmas.*

As we rode back through town, I couldn't help thinking that it looked like a toy village on a lake made out of a mirror, with lights flickering everywhere. The snow was so white and the lights shimmered so playfully. The lake was already covered with a sheet of ice and the houses around the lake were all lit up and cozy looking.

Back at the firehouse, the first crew was busy putting their rig back in order. As we rode in, I called us back to a holiday mood.

"Mahopac Falls EMS 19-7-1 to 40 control."

"Go ahead 19-7-1"

"Mahopac Falls 19-7-1 is back in service and back in quarters. Merry Christmas fellas!"

The Sheriff's office didn't answer. You're not supposed to say things like that on the emergency frequency. But it was Christmas and I was starting to feel good again.

Tony had been shaken by the call he was on. I invited him back to my place for a cup of coffee and a chat. We sat at my kitchen table and talked about why things happen the way they do. Sometimes, after a bad call, firefighters want to sit down with somebody else and talk. I guess that's the human need for confession and storytelling that is found in every culture in every age. So we drank coffee and talked. Tony had had a tough night and now I was once again incapable of getting up. We talked about the call, what went right, what we could have done better, and what we had learned. Eventually we started to talk about Christmas, and for some reason I started to remember Christmas when I was a kid. Tony was just a year or two older than I was. We had come from that same point in time. When you remember the same songs, you share many of the same memories. I started to tell him about some of the memories I had from the fifties, when I had been a child. The memories flooded over me. I remembered my father, whom I wouldn't see again in this life. I remembered growing up with many brothers and sisters in an upstairs apartment. I shared a bedroom with two other brothers, and we could never sleep on Christmas Eve. I remembered a plate of cookies for Santa that was always empty in the morning. I remembered the gleam of new bicycles and the rattle of games and models inside brightly colored paper. One year, one of us even claimed to have heard sleigh bells in the dark of a snowy night. Looking back, I realized that my parents hadn't had a lot then; we just never knew it. After a while, Tony and I said goodnight, and Tony headed home to his family for Christmas. I prayed that there would be no more calls that night. I went up to my bedroom. The television was still on and *A Christmas Carol* was just about over. Scrooge had gone to his nephew's house seeking forgiveness and had won the hearts of Bob Cratchet and Tiny Tim. For some reason I was more receptive to this than usual. A tear came to my eye. I don't know whether I was crying for Tiny Tim, for that family in our town that had just been struck by tragedy, or for myself. Memories began to pour over me. I remembered some of my Christmas disappointments. I remembered a lonely Christmas far from home. I thought of all of those friends and loved ones who had been lost in the great river of time. I began to cry for all of the sad Christmases I remembered.

I guess I had reached my limit. I held up my pager and took the batteries out. I settled down in my old, comfortable bed and turned out the lights. Outside the window the neighbors' Christmas lights lit up the night. I felt safe that night. It's the security you feel when you've done what you're supposed to and you can sleep with a clear conscience. If I had not made it to my feet a little while earlier, that Christmas morning would not have felt so right.

Some people get really wound up about which gifts they give or get. But this can miss the point of why we give gifts at all. The best gifts are those that can be given over and over again every day. They cost us nothing because they come from our heart.

The story of Scrooge is a story of redemption and forgiveness. It tells us that it is never too late to change and it is never to late to love. It shows us that miracles are possible even when we think they are out of reach. Scrooge dragged himself out of bed on a snowy Christmas long ago only to find out that what is important is not how much you get but how much you give. For it is only in giving that we truly receive.

13

Style, or how to exhibit grace under pressure

Style is the hallmark of a temperament stamped on the material at hand

André Maurois

The hot rod was going over seventy miles an hour when the teenage driver lost control coming around a curve. He hit the brakes, and the burning rubber left smoke and skid marks before the car veered off the road and became airborne. It sheared down one telephone pole and wrapped itself around a second. It landed with a thunderous crash upside-down, smoking. The doors had been crushed shut and a limp body hung silently inside. Someone who lived across the street called the Carmel Police. Dispatcher Mike Johnson got on the air and called the Mahopac Falls ambulance for a personal injury auto accident (PIAA). It was a muggy, seventy-degree June night around six o'clock. The sun was setting in hues of crimson and purple as the sky was growing dark. None of us knew it at that time but this call would be a test of our character.

The German philosopher, Friedrich Nietzsche, was very interested in the idea of "character". He lived and wrote at the end of the nineteenth century, a time when many traditions had begun to be questioned. It is he who is most remembered for the statement, "God is Dead." But it was not just God that Nietzsche wanted to free himself from. He thought that Plato had betrayed us by placing too much faith in another world beyond this one. Neitzsche disliked saints who looked more towards heaven than earth. He questioned a religion such as Hinduism, which denied the body and its pleasures. He even doubted the rationalism and optimism of science. He thought that life was not as logical as science made it out to be. He wondered if science would solve all of the problems it was attacking. He thought that life was more complex and many-faceted than any one simple theory could encompass.

With so many ideals and traditional beliefs taken away, what would people be left with? What could the philosopher still pin his hopes on? To answer this dilemma, Nietzsche imagined a type of new person who would come and change the world. He called this person the "Uebermensch," which has been translated as the "Superman" or, more accurately, the "Overman." This "Overman" would be free of superstition and fear. He wouldn't be hindered by false ideals or misplaced loyalties. He would be clear-eyed and self-aware. Most of all, he would have what Nietzsche called "style." Style for Nietzsche was that element, which makes the ordinary into the extraordinary, that which turns any day into a holiday, that which lifts ordinary life to a higher level. Nietzsche wanted to transform human life into a work of art. He hoped that the people themselves would become the painter's canvass or the sculptor's stone.

He wanted people to live in such a way as to show grace and courage in every situation. Even when life was at its most difficult, Nietzsche's "Uebermensch" or "new person" would live with "style."

The call was up on S.... Road, not too far from the church on the hill. I responded with the ambulance and arrived at the accident site with Tony Luccaro and Dougie Hyatt, one of the old-timers. We got there before the police car arrived. We could see the car twisted around the body of the teenager inside. It was the most gruesome sight I'd seen since I'd joined the department and I winced a little. I wished someone else were there instead of me. Tony got on the radio and called for the rescue truck and the special equipment required for the most serious vehicle accidents—the Jaws of Life.

At times like this, the pressure is on the jaws crew. Firefighters who have been around know what a "jaws call" means. It's usually a matter of life and death. It means we have to work fast and we have to work smart. There is no margin for error and no second chance. When a jaws call comes over the radio, it usually means that someone is trapped inside the twisted metal of an auto wreck, that that person is injured, and that the metal has to be pried apart to get the victim out. This whole process is called "extrication". In addition the firefighters are performing this act on a kind of stage. There is always an audience of interested bystanders at a jaws call. It's a real test of character.

I was in that difficult situation now.

Tony leaned in through the car window and started giving first aid. We got an oxygen mask on the victim and stopped the bleeding from the wounds we could reach. We waited for the rescue truck and the jaws to arrive.

The jaws are also known as the "Hurst tool," after one of the companies that manufactures them. The jaws are hooked up to a pump that provides hydraulic pressure to them. They look like big scissors and each of their two tips can exert thousands of pounds of force. The rescue truck also carries other tools for extrication. One is called "the Ajax tool." This is a cutting instrument operated on pressurized air, which can open the roof of a car like a can of sardines. Another is the Hurst "cutters." It has two sharp blades and it works on hydraulic power. It can cut the doorposts on a car so that the roof can be peeled back. It is also used to cut a steering wheel if a person is trapped behind it.

A lot of manpower is needed at a jaws call. People are needed to hold the car steady using blocks of wood called "cribbing;" others are needed to set up lights if it is dark; to make sure all of the generators are running correctly and to put out our tools. A few of our members are jaws experts, although a lot of us are trained to use them in a pinch. The two most likely to get a call are Gary Link and Tommy Stasiak. Gary is a car guy and knows car bodies inside and out. He knows where the strong points are and where the weak points are. He knows all about latches, and the best place to "pop a door," as he puts it. There is something about using such sharp power tools so close to human flesh that focuses the mind. When operating the Hurst tool, rescuers have to work fast and carefully. They are on a tight schedule, and with an injured victim inside that metal, it's crucial not to push the metal the wrong way. Firefighters say the jaws are a one-man tool. But more than one person is needed to work them best because it weighs sixty-five pounds and must be pushed constantly against the weight of the car. Anyone who's been on the jaws during a call will feel it in their arms for days.

That night, Gary Link and Tommy showed up to work the jaws. Gary is the most mechanical guy I know. When I saw Gary and

Stasiak, I breathed a sigh of relief because they were experts. Before starting with the jaws, they made an incision near the door lock with an axe so they could get the tips inside. One person holds the pry bar inside the seam while another firefighter hammers at it with an axe. If at all possible, the tips should go in where the lock is so that the door can be popped right there.

By this time, the fire engine had arrived with a charged hose line in case the car caught fire. When a car is so badly crushed, fire is always a possibility. There were firefighters everywhere and a crowd had gathered across the street. The jaws were then hooked up to the generator and brought to the car. Gary and Tommy had their turnout gear on and the visors were down on their helmets. Metal can fly when the pressure of the jaws is put to it. Someone working the jaws always has to lean into the tool because it is always squeezing out against him.

Gary and Tommy lifted the jaws and stuck them into the hole in the door. The jaws whined loudly as the tool opened its mouth. I could hear the crunching and crackling of the metal as it broke and gave way. All of a sudden, there was a "pop!"—the jaws pop out frequently and then they have to be stuck back in at another angle. More sounds of whining and breaking metal followed and then another pop. The door opened and Gary and Tommy pulled it off.

There was now another problem. The dashboard was crushing the victim's legs and the steering wheel was in his chest. By attaching a chain to the steering column, Gary and Tommy were able to use a second Hurst tool to pull up the steering column and dashboard. The teenager, who was semi-conscious and bleeding, was awake now and screaming. Gary and Tommy kept going. In a few seconds, the boy was free. We put an extrication collar on him to keep his neck straight in case of spinal injury and rolled him out of the car and onto a backboard and then onto a stretcher. We backed up and lifted the stretcher into the rear of the ambulance. The teenager was in bad shape. Nobody was sure he was going to survive. There were more than enough people to help in the back of the ambulance. Camille was in there with Jack Casey so I stayed behind. Gary and Tommy were sitting by the side of the road, covered with sweat.

The boy's injuries were severe but they weren't fatal. Both legs were broken and some of his ribs weren't where they should have been. We were happy to find out later that his internal organs were not damaged. He was on crutches for a while but now I see him shopping in Red Mills Market and he seems okay. I know who he is but he doesn't know me. I don't think he remembers anything about that night.

I once asked Tony Luccaro if he ever had the urge to go up to somebody whose life he had helped save and introduce himself. He smiled. "I always figured that was something they'd rather forget, so I don't mention it."

I always follow Tony's advice. I still see that youngster from time to time. Once I opened the door for him and his mother when they were going into Red Mills Market. I smiled and he smiled back. He wasn't aware that I know his guardian angels, Tommy and Gary.

Most fire departments and rescue squads in America today carry the Jaws of Life. Most rural fire departments have jaws drills a few times a year. They take old abandoned cars and practice cutting them up so that their skills will be sharp when it comes to the real thing. They practice ways to break a window with someone inside. They practice removing a windshield and cutting people out of cars that are upside-down or on their sides. Car wrecks aren't usually simple textbook cases. Each wreck is bent and shaped in a unique way. Sometimes the car is on its roof. Other times it is perched up on one side. Sometimes the doors are so mangled that another way into the car is needed. Extrication is as much of an art as it is a science.

Not all jaws calls involve automobiles, however. I was up at the fire department in Patterson, NY, looking at its new ambulance some time ago, and some of the rescue people up there told me that they had had a few unusual calls that required extrication. Once, a young girl had got her hand stuck inside the round inkwell of one of those old desks they still have in the school up there and the fire department got called to extricate her. A few weeks earlier, someone had gone after a ball in the pocket of a pool table in the One Buck Inn in downtown Patterson and had needed the fire department to get his arm out. That call was traumatic for some of the firefighters—it was the only good pool table for ten miles around. Our most unusual jaws call at the Falls came one New Year's Eve when we had to pry a tree apart so that a dog could get its paw out.

The department nearest to us is Putnam Valley (or as we call it, "Put Valley.") Part of the territory it covers is the Taconic State Parkway, a long, twisting, heavily traveled road that freezes regularly in cold weather. The accidents there keep Put Valley hopping, so they use the jaws frequently. Put Valley has only two ambulances. We have a mutual-aid arrangement with them so that we can call on each other in times of need. On weekdays, when manpower is short, they often call on us if they get jaws calls on the Taconic State Parkway.

A while back, we were over there for a serious affair. There is a side street on the border of Put Valley and Mahopac Falls that crosses the parkway. A car going across it had been hit broadside by a vehicle traveling at high speed on the Taconic. A third car then had been unable to stop and had slammed into the first two.

I was at home grading papers. The radio was tuned to WHUD and Johnnie Rivers was singing *Secret Agent Man*. Suddenly the tones went off, signaling that we were needed for mutual aid. I was looking for an excuse not to grade those papers anyway, so off I went. (The only thing worse than taking exams is trying to correct them. Instructors don't like tests either!) I was out the door and in the car in just a few seconds. At the station, I jumped into the ambulance and took off with Jack Casey and Tony Luccaro. About a mile from the firehouse, we heard that it was a jaws call, and it sounded like a serious one.

When we arrived, there was no traffic going north or south on the parkway. I had to weave past cars and the wreckage to get close enough to park the ambulance. The Put Valley people were all there. Helena Brown, their ambulance captain was on the scene and in charge. The Put Valley Ambulance Corps had many members at the site. One of their EMTs was reaching inside the car trying to reassure the patient. Tony went over and started to help get the door off. Jack and I got the stretcher in close and waited.

The jaws had done their work, but the door was still not off. We all took hold of the door and grunted as we rocked and pulled. Eventually, there was a snap and the door came off. We got inside and removed the driver and I drove to the hospital in overdrive. We had all made it through.

He was an elderly man, but he wasn't as badly injured as we had first thought. On the way to the hospital he talked to us about gardening. It was one of the more pleasant rides I had taken that week. I also remember that particular call because since then, whenever it rains, my aching back has told me that yanking on that door hadn't been such a good idea.

I've often seen character and courage in emergencies. I've seen people take a hose line and crawl forward on all fours into a building where fire is raging and they can't see a thing. I've seen people climb up onto icy roofs over raging fires, take saws and start cutting holes in roofs to ventilate fires. People do these things because they know they have to.

If courage is, as Hemingway wrote, "grace under pressure," my vote goes to those people who are jaws operators as the embodiment of it. Each time, the twist in the metal is different. Each time, there are different problems. Each time, they're on the spot, and there is no one else they can call to help them. Tonight or tomorrow, when the rescue truck is called to a motor vehicle accident in the Falls, Tommy, Tony, or Gary Link will be there and will demonstrate, once again, how to be graceful under pressure.

This "grace under pressure" is the truest example to me of what Friedrich Nietzsche called "style." When the pressure is on, lives are on the line and nothing can be taken for granted, many people might panic. There are some people I know who shine their brightest in those moments.

I'm not sure that if Friedrich Nietzsche walked into the Mahopac Falls firehouse, he would recognize my friends as examples of the "Overman" he talked so much about. And I know that most of my friends still live by many of the traditional values that Nietzsche thought were outdated. As far as I am concerned though, when the chips are down and we're up against a life-and-death challenge, it takes style to want to be the one on the trigger, to face the challenge smoothly, and make it look easy. That's the style that rescuers show working the jaws.

Years after the Putnam Valley rescue, I showed up at a jaws call where a very vocal woman was trapped inside of a luxury sports car. She wasn't injured too badly but the doors were crushed and she could not get out without our assistance. She was screaming at us to watch the paint. She kept telling us how much the car cost. At that point, Stasiak showed up with the rescue truck and began to take out the jaws. I smiled at her. "Don't worry ma'am, we are trained professionals."

Then I turned to Stasiak and winked. He rolled his eyes as he fired up the jaws. As he approached the door he said to me, "Pal, this is why you should never own a car that costs more than my house!"

At this point the woman was crying. "My beautiful car!" I smiled and realized something she was not thinking about at that time. She was in a car and the jaws were being used. It could have been worse, much worse.

14

Death, or how to treasure every day

Death cancels everything but truth; and strips a man of everything but genius and virtue. It is a sort of natural canonization. It makes the meanest of us sacred— it installs the poet in his immortality, and lifts him to the skies.

William Hazlitt

A thousand years ago, in a far away eastern land, an enlightened Zen master wanted to tell his disciples to live every moment to the fullest. He didn't want them to spend their lives asleep while the world, with all of its colors and scents, went on without them. So he tried to awaken them with this saying: "They say that those who kill are murderers. But what of those who live as if they are asleep? Are they not murderers? Are they not killing time?"

We all remember some moments when we were fully awake and fully alive. We remember our first kiss. We remember the night we graduated from high school or lost a loved one. Imagine feeling that connected and focused at almost every moment— that's what being fully awake is like.

From time to time, people experience moments that change their lives. For some, it is a gaze, for others, it might be a word. Dante saw Beatrice only a few times in his long life and never spoke a word to her. But she moved him to write *The Divine Comedy*, one of the great works of literature. Her silent beauty inspired a lifetime of artistic creation. Any moment can be such a moment; we need only be attentive enough to see it.

A moment when life hangs in the balance can heal. It can mend souls that are hurt and put things back in perspective. This is true for both the sick or injured person and those who are there to help. Being present at this moment could change a person's life one way, or the other. Someone who rides the ambulance regularly will have some very intense experiences. Most ambulance calls, like most fire calls, are "routine"; that is, they are routine for us, not for the people having the crisis. Frequently someone is having difficulty breathing or experiencing chest pains, and we transport that person to the hospital without incident. They are safe and we don't have to get too excited. Every now and then though, you can go to help someone and experience something that sticks in your memory or that even changes your life. Any ambulance call might be the one that changes your life. So even though many of our calls are "routine," we try to treat each one with the attention and speed that keeps the situation from getting worse.

I've done CPR in the back of a moving ambulance a number of times, but the first time that I did it still stands out to me. It began about ten o'clock on a hot, humid July day. A middle-aged woman had had a heart attack. The call from Sergeant Mike Johnson first came over as "a women with chest pains," but shortly afterward it changed to indicate that she was having a full-blown heart attack. And yes, he managed to tell us this with his usual dreamy indifference that keeps us all so calm.

I raced to the firehouse and saw Jack Casey get out of his car and jump into the back of the ambulance just ahead of me. My car screeched to a stop and I jumped into the passenger seat next to him. I got on the radio and called us out en route to the scene. Mike Johnson got on the air again and told us to respond "forthwith." We knew that he meant that the situation was urgent, so we stepped on it. With lights and sirens blazing, we sailed over the roads, racing against the clock.

A few minutes later, we pulled up to the scene as a frantic young woman ran out of the door screaming. We took the oxygen, the bag valve mask, and all our other supplies, and ran from the rig just as it was rolling to a stop. In our safety classes we emphasize that one should never open the door of a moving vehicle before it has come to a full stop. Sometimes, though, when seconds count we stretch the rules and rush just a tad. What's taught in the classroom and practiced at drills is important, but sometimes we have to improvise when a life might be on the line.

We got inside to find a heavy, middle-aged women lying lifeless on the floor. She was wearing a simple plaid dress and slippers. From the color of her arms and face I could tell she had little or no circulation. Her skin was a blue gray. Jack felt for a pulse in her neck. He listened for breath; then he looked up at me frantically and said, "No pulse, no respiration."

Jack tilted the woman's head back to make sure the airway into her lungs was open and delivered two short blasts of air with the bag valve mask in the hope that the oxygen would get her breathing. Sometimes the simple act of sending a breath or two into a person's lungs can start his or her breathing again. Today we were not so lucky. He listened again and looked at me. He shook his head "no" before he spoke.

"Start CPR!"

The woman's daughter was crying and screaming. Neighbors were rushing in from all directions as I locked my elbows and began chest compressions. Jack called the strokes and gave a burst of air for every five compressions I did. One of the Carmel police officers who was on the scene helped our driver bring in the stretcher with the CPR board under it. As soon as they were in place, Jack was ready to move. We stopped CPR for a few seconds as we picked up the woman and got ready to lift her up onto the stretcher. Jack looked me dead in the eyes.

"On my count of three, we lift!"

Jack counted and we lifted the woman onto the stretcher. We began to roll it toward the ambulance as I continued the chest compressions and Jack gave her oxygen. With the intense physical strain of doing CPR, time seemed to flow more slowly. After what seemed like an eternity, we reached the back of the ambulance. Again we stopped for a second as we all grabbed a bottom rail of the stretcher. Jack counted to three and we lifted the woman up into the ambulance. We jumped inside and began CPR again. The woman's daughter wanted to get into the back with us, but there was no room and no time, so the police officer asked a neighbor to drive her and follow us. Then the officer closed the doors and tapped the side of the ambulance to let the driver know that we were ready to go. Jack took over the chest compressions. After trying to push air into the woman's lungs for just ten minutes, I was already exhausted. That's what happens to a middle-aged college professor on a CPR call.

The ambulance took off and, with the siren wailing nonstop, we sped down the country roads as fast as we could to the hospital. Even though the ambulance has air conditioning, the effort of trying to revive the woman was making the back of the ambulance very humid and uncomfortable. That was the least of our worries. The woman still wasn't responding. I was giving oxygen and waiting to take another turn at the chest compressions as soon as Jack told me he was tired and wanted to switch places.

At that moment, something happened that I will never forget, something seemingly unimportant but filled with meaning for me. As I wiped the sweat from my face, I happened to look out the ambulance window at the world outside. We were passing by Lake Mahopac. The water was blue and shimmering. The sky had just a few billowy summertime clouds. The greenery was thick and dark. At that moment, I was struck by the sharp contrast between our frantic efforts to save this woman's life and the serene tranquility of the lake. The beauty of the lake was timeless. We, however, are temporal creatures, and for us that day, time was running out.

We took turns doing compressions as the ride went on. The ambulance rocked from side to side as we sped through town and raced against the clock. It's very demanding to keep CPR up for more than twenty minutes, and every second counts. I was still fairly new to the CPR process and Jack guided me carefully. Each of our members is CPR certified. As I was finding out, carrying a card in one's wallet and actually performing CPR in a real, life-threatening situation are very different. Right then, our ambulance run was looking like a bad one. When someone dies in the back of an ambulance, or as EMS workers say, "goes sour," it is hard to go on another ambulance call. It shakes you up with the fear that it might happen again. Those are moments an ambulance crew doesn't forget.

We still weren't getting any pulse. The driver yelled back "We're 30 seconds from touchdown!" The ambulance pulled into Putnam Hospital. We leaped out and continued CPR right into the emergency room. When the nurses took over, Jack and I sat down panting. Jack put his hands in his white hair and looked at me. We had been so totally immersed in the moment that we had had no time to reflect or hesitate. The woman was lifeless and gray as the team began its intervention. I felt that our efforts had been in vain and all of our work had been for nothing. Little could I have guessed how this story would have a surprise ending.

Amazingly enough, our patient survived. I went to church the next day, expecting to hear the priest say we should pray for the souls of the newly departed. When he said that we should pray for the sick and mentioned the name of the woman we had taken to the hospital, I was stunned. After mass, I went to the priest and asked if there had been some mistake. He said there had not been, that he had been with the woman a few hours earlier. I called Jack, in shock. He was as surprised as I was. We found out that when the woman arrived at Putnam Hospital, the staff used all of their skill and knowledge to get her heart beating and her lungs working. The CPR we had done had kept her alive until we got to the hospital. We had bought time and cheated death. Art Brady knew the woman. In his volunteer role at Putnam Hospital he visited her a few days later in the Intensive Care Unit. She was in good enough condition by then to tell him to thank us.

Our ambulance has made a lot of CPR calls since that hot summer day. I've done CPR dozens of times and have a better idea now of what to do and what not to do. Like everything else, proper CPR technique takes time. Most CPR calls don't turn out as well as my first. The vast majority of the time, the odds are against success and the ambulance crew is hoping against hope, fighting a losing battle with death. When we lose, we can never feel good, even when we know from the beginning that the effort is probably hopeless.

CPR calls are very special for me. Each one makes the world new for me all over again. I look at flowers differently and I see butterflies and birds that I wouldn't otherwise have noticed. I take a deep breath and know that breathing will not always come that easily to me. One day, perhaps one day soon, it will be gone, like a breeze that appears out of nowhere and suddenly stops, or like a red and gold butterfly that briefly shows its glory before disappearing forever.

I've learned that the key moments in a firefighter's life are not just while fighting a fire or trying to save someone's life. They also come when I pay attention to my truck or when I make sure all of the equipment is ready. They come when I rack the hose so that it will be ready for the initial attack. They come as a part of the way I treat every human being at every minute of every day. For a firefighter and for everyone, each moment is a key moment. Every beat of someone's heart is a miracle. There is an old song that tells us to appreciate every thing because we will not be here one hundred years from today. It puts things in a different, more sympathetic, light.

Yes, one hundred years from today, you and I will probably not be here. Sometimes I sit by the rippling waters of Lake Mahopac and watch the clouds forming and coming apart as they drift in the blue sky over the lake. I think to myself how temporal they are and how beautiful. We should live each second that will never come again.

The world should be thankful that Beatrice walked down that street in Florence centuries ago, and it should also be thankful that at a window stood a man named Dante who was enlightened enough to understand what a moment can bring.

15

Tradition, or how to preserve things worth keeping

Tradition simply means that we need to end what began well and continue what is worth continuing.

José Bergamin

We live in a world where nothing can be counted on for very long. When things break we no longer fix them, we throw them away and get new ones. This throw away attitude has extended far beyond television sets and radios. It has extended to how we treat each other and what we are willing to hang on to. It is hard to know what to give up and what is worth keeping.

The British political philosopher Edmund Burke was a conservative. When he was alive, the French Revolution broke out. People took to the streets and declared a new age. They wanted a new religion, a new government, and even a new calendar. Burke wasn't caught up in all of the hysteria that surrounded the

French Revolution, though. He thought that institutions that had lasted a long time had some inner strength that might be lost. He was a man who knew the importance of tradition as the glue that keeps a community together. He knew that the subcultures in a society, each with its own customs, create the foundation for the larger social order.

There are many subcultures in any town. There are garden clubs, chess clubs, little leagues, and book clubs. People like activities that give their lives structure. I have some good friends that don't feel the need to be part of organizations, but I've always been a joiner. One of the activities I loved most was coaching my son and daughter all through little league in the Mahopac Sports Association. I coached baseball, softball, soccer, football, and basketball. I was there for the highs and the lows with my little Brandon and Kelly as we won and lost and grew up together. I often stood on the sidelines amazed at how none of what we learned in practice was evident on the field during the games.

Some traditions are worth being part of. There are many traditions in my town and the fire department has a few of its own. Last December, I was standing in a deli waiting to get a cup of coffee when I overheard two people saying that the holidays weren't what they used to be. One fellow said it didn't "feel like" the holidays that year. I wanted to tell them that if they had been with me the Saturday before, they would have felt the holiday spirit just as intensely as when they were children. Every year our fire department, like many others, hosts Santa as he rides through the town giving out candy canes and shaking hands with little children. This tradition goes back decades. The whole operation is something to see. We order almost a thousand candy canes and brochures on holiday fire safety. We wax and polish our trucks so that they'll look presentable to our neighbors. We publish our route in the local paper and post it in the windows of the Red Mills Market. Some truck foremen even tie big red bows around the front of their engines to give the trucks a festive look. The whole event is called the "Candy Cane Run."

Around eleven o'clock in the morning, the firefighters start to gather at the firehouse. Four trucks go out and through the special magic of the Falls fire department, each truck has a Santa who gives out the canes. Every year we go into the attic, which holds all of the fire department memorabilia, to get out the four Santa suits. One qualification for the job of Santa is that he must have his own natural padding, so the big guys usually get the job. Each truck is loaded with people who will go past their own homes and neighbors. The driver has to go slowly and to know when Santa wants to jump down, run into a house, and jump back on. Believe me, hopping on and off the fire truck is hard work for Santa!

Because all the trucks are out in different parts of the district, Dougie Hyatt, one of our old-timers, stays on the base radio to make sure everyone is in touch in case there is a fire. One year we had an ambulance call at the beginning of the run and two of us had to run a quarter mile back to the firehouse to make the first ambulance out. The dispatcher makes sure he knows where all the trucks are and if we are running low on candy canes.

By twelve o'clock, all the trucks are lined up with their engines running. Once our captain gives us the sign to go, the Santas start waving, the helpers grab handfuls of brochures and candy canes, and the trucks roll out with their sirens wailing and lights flashing. Santa's helper, who rides shotgun, uses the truck's PA system to sound out a hardy "Ho Ho Ho, Merry Christmas, Merry Christmas!"

The children gather in big groups in some of the housing developments. The firefighters have even been known to take a detour for a child who is too sick to go outside. The Candy Cane Runs have been great fun over the past decades, and a lot of lore surrounds the old days. Of course, in those days the attitude towards drinking was a lot more liberal. The firefighters would start off with a few shots of whiskey at the firehouse, then would stop at many houses along the way for some eggnog and what they used to call "antifreeze." Needless to say, Santa was in a much better mood at the end of the run than he was at the beginning. But time and tides change, so we no longer use "antifreeze." There is no drinking before or during our run. Today, we are not as much fun as we used to be, but we are much safer. There was a time, twenty years ago when a fire was called in during the Candy Cane Run. We still have an old newspaper photo of Santa on the roof with the firefighters trying to put out a burning chimney. We still run the same route, with the same trucks, and a lot of the same people that rode years ago.

Recently we've added another tradition. We combine our Candy Cane Run with the U.S. Marine's Toys for Tots. This is a program sponsored by the Marines that collects new unwrapped toys and gives them to boys and girls who might otherwise get nothing for the holidays. The firefighters distribute leaflets for weeks, asking people to have a toy for Santa. It's a way of giving thanks, we suggest, for all of the blessings they have. As our Santas are giving out candy canes, they are also collecting toys. The trucks roll through the town filling up with toys and packages. Some people use the Candy Cane Run to show us how much they appreciate our work. They invite us for some eggnog or give us homemade cookies as we drive by. We have a great time, hanging in the air off those freezing trucks in the middle of December, watching the youngsters faces light up when they hear the siren and see Santa. Fire trucks are dramatic things to children. They're so big and loud that they make Santa more believable when he shows up in one. The big trucks go so slowly, so you would think the line of cars behind them would start honking or complaining. For the most part they don't; they know what season it is, too. When the Candy Cane Run is done, the firefighters head back to the firehouse for some hot chili and cocoa. That's the traditional fare at the end of the candy cane run every year. Jack Casey has made the chili every year for decades, and nobody else knows the recipe. It's a day that I try not to miss.

There are a number of other traditions at the Falls. We have a Christmas dance every year and this year we invited the whole community to a caroling and a tree lighting. We served coffee and hot chocolate and sang songs in the chilly night air. The Falls also gave out twenty-five food baskets for Christmas dinner to those who needed them and bought clothes for the twenty-five neediest children in our hamlet. There's need everywhere, no matter where you live. Need knows no season.

Remembering how those two fellows in the deli were complaining about how the holidays were not what they used to be, I thought, "Next year, I'll invite those two along on my truck."

Winter isn't the only time for tradition at the Falls. One of the most important traditions for local fire departments involves parades. In a parade, firefighters can dress up, shine their equipment, and show the community who they are. Many people in the community see the fire trucks rushing past their houses only once or twice a year. The local parades are our chance to say hello to our friends and neighbors and let them see how their taxes are being spent.

Parade season takes a great deal of planning. We have a Parade Marshall who has to plan almost a year in advance which parades we'll march in and what band we'll hire. Every fire department has a band that it pays to walk in front of its marchers and trucks. We've had the same one for years. The band is called "O.

H. Booth," and the members look like colonial soldiers, with long hair and stubble beards. They play some rousing Sousa marches and join us for a beer when the parade is finished.

Once the arrangements are made, we have to get the trucks ready for parade season. Many nights are spent taking out every screw on the parade trucks and polishing them. Every compartment is cleaned and the undersides of the trucks are made spotless. The hose is racked tight and neat. During the parades, the fire trucks of each department are judged, with the judges noting every detail as we pass the reviewing area.

The Falls has not done that well in parades for the last few years. Our neighboring department, the Mahopac Fire Department, wins trophy after trophy and is one of the best parade companies in the state. This has always been a sore point with some of the Falls firefighters, who don't think that ceremonial parades are such a big deal. I remember Tommy Stasiak once telling me, "We're not here to look pretty. We're here to fight fires!"

Even though the guys at the Falls get really mad at me when I speak up, I don't really agree with this view. I think that there's a good deal to learn from a company like Mahopac. There's something to be said for looking so good and focusing your energy on a single effort. There are many ways to show excellence and motivation and parades are one of them.

Parades involve many traditions and established roles. For twenty years, Charlie Locke drove the chief's car in parades. The Link brothers have carried our Department banner for the past twelve years. The chief always walks in front, carrying a brass trumpet with flowers inside, a reminder of past times when the chief used to yell instructions to the firefighters through a trumpet. We even have a few new traditions. For a few years I was in the color guard with several other members. The color guard consists of an American flag flanked by two members marching ahead of the department, carrying axes with shining chrome heads. This represents our ability to serve and protect. The axes are never used other than for that one purpose. One year we even won the award for best color guard in a parade. We march no matter what the weather brings. Once a member commits to marching, we expect him or her to go unless there's a big fire. (Our department always leaves an ambulance crew and a fire-fighting crew back at the station so that the district is not stripped of protection.)

At parade time, all the other fire departments are lined up and we visit with our friends from the Carmel, Lake Carmel, and Brewster Departments. It's funny seeing them in dress uniforms with their hair combed. Usually when we meet, it's three o'clock in the morning, our shoes are on the wrong feet and there's no time to socialize. That's one of the good things about parades. We get a chance to visit with people whom we've worked with under pressure and whose names we may not even know.

Eventually, the parade begins. The parade marshal always yells at me to make sure the color guard is in a straight line. The trucks start up, the marchers get in line and O. H. Booth starts the drumbeat. The Parade Marshall walks alongside of us, yelling things like, "Doc" you're out of step!" "Luccaro, put your hat on the right way!" "Stasiak, stop waving!" He does the best he can to keep us in line, but it's hard to maintain iron discipline at an event like this.

I like parades. I like the color and the day outdoors, and I like the children clapping as we march by. I am proud of the Falls fire department. We deserve the acclaim.

Two parades that the firefighters in my department especially like are the annual parade in Patterson and our own Memorial Day Parade on the lake in Mahopac. The parade in Patterson is wonderful because of the scenery. Patterson is even more remote and rural than Mahopac Falls. It is a woodsy place, nestled in hills that seem to roll around it. The air is alive with sounds of chirping birds and the sounds of summer in the country. It has a wonderful Main Street. There are old churches with little cemeteries on both sides of the walk. There is a bar called the "One Buck Inn" that has been there a good long time. It has been a favorite of area firefighters for many years. There are old houses with wrap-around porches and swings. Old folks sit on their porches in rocking chairs waving little American flags and smiling as we pass. Children hold balloons and clap. Being there is like marching back in time. For a few hours, we live in the world that people always tell me has gone, but that on this special day, seems to be still with us.

My favorite parade is the Memorial Day Parade in downtown Mahopac. Because every town has its own Memorial Day Parade, the only two departments that attend are Mahopac and Mahopac Falls. One year my daughter, Kelly, marched with the Girl Scouts, I marched with the fire department, and my son, Brandon, carried the wreath for the Boy Scouts. We don't march very far. We start at Clark Place and march about half a mile down Route 6. Then we turn onto East Lake Boulevard and come to attention. There, behind the library, by the old Methodist Church on the lake, is Memorial Park. It consists of a rock with a brass plaque on it and an old oak tree that was planted seventy years ago in memory of the Mahopac residents who died in World War I. The monument overlooks the lake and oftentimes there is a strong breeze there. It is surrounded by a little stonewall with a gravel path leading into the monument.

We stand there in the sun and listen to heartfelt speeches by veterans and invocations by our local rabbi, ministers, and Catholic priest. Sometimes the speeches are tearful as the old veterans recall the battles of years past. Often times there are memories shared and stories told about the bravery of the men and women of Mahopac in wars past. After we dedicate wreaths and listen to the high school band play the Star Spangled Banner, we all walk down to the VFW post, where beer is on tap, soda is cold, and hot dogs are cooking. The VFW post is located right on the lake. So if the weather is fine, as it usually is on that day, we stand outside in the sun with a hot dog in one hand and beer in the other. After a long winter, Memorial Day is the day that summer really begins for us.

The bartender at the VFW is an old friend of mine. His name is Rudy Horvath. As a young man he landed on D-Day and now not only keeps the VFW spiffy, but is a member of our fire department. Every Memorial Day he takes his place behind the bar, wearing his VFW hat and a Memorial Day paper poppy on his uniform.

As we arrive, the Post Commander greets people on behalf of the post. Almost everyone in town is there. I stand with the firefighters, the police, my fellow coaches and parents from the Mahopac Sports Association and all of the other characters from town. We all stand there by the side of the lake, watching the clouds float over the water, sipping beer and visiting with each other. This year I stood inside the bar and listened to the radio playing Martha and the Vandellas *Heat wave.*

Later, many of the Falls firefighters will go up to a party that is held at the local American Legion Hall on Buck's Hollow Road. There are picnics and boating throughout the day. I have sometimes gone out on Lake Mahopac in a friend's boat and anchored in the waters off Canopus Island. The sun is warm that time of year, but the water is still refreshingly cold. I think Memorial Day, with townspeople sharing their memories and their friendship, has helped me better understand everything that's good about America.

There is one last part of Memorial Day that cannot be forgotten. Tradition has it that on this day a flag is placed on the grave of every Mahopac Falls firefighter within driving distance. For decades, Tony Luccaro and Art Brady have seen that this gets done. Last year was the first time that I was given the honor of taking part in this ritual. Walt Swarm went along for the ride. He not only knows every cemetery, but he knows where members were buried fifty years ago and can walk right up to their grave. The directions he gives, though, are what you would expect: they're clear to him but not to anyone else. He usually says something like, "Find the big elm tree and it is just south of there." So even though Walt was there, I was given a map to help find the gravestones. He and I drove to a small cemetery not too far away and carried a little American flag into the graveyard. When I found the marker, I sat down for a minute. I never knew this person, but he was a firefighter and knew and loved the Falls fire department, just as I do now. I touched the stone and it felt cool. The sun was hot and the spring grass over the grave was bright green. I pushed the flag into the grave and stood up. Next year another flag would be placed in front of that stone. This tradition will continue as long as the Mahopac Falls Volunteer Fire Department exists.

The Falls has a tradition about everything. When a member dies there are a number of rituals that take place. First, an announcement comes over our pagers: "It is with deep regret that we announce the passing of…" and then they say his or her name. The Department will assemble in uniform for the wake on Thursday at seven p.m. in the main station. We assemble and go in our uniforms and white gloves to the funeral home. We march in and stand in silence. The chief usually says a few words and Tony Luccaro reads the Twenty-Third Psalm: "The Lord is my Shepherd, I shall not want...." We pray by the casket, give our condolences to the family and head back to the fire department. If the deceased is someone we all knew well, we sometimes open the bar and toast our friend as he or she goes on the journey home.

At the next monthly meeting, we stand in silence for a minute. We hear "Last call for firefighter (and here they will say his or her name.)" and Tony Luccaro rings the bell, muffling the sound. Our brother or sister will not answer another call and it is we who are left to serve and protect.

Many people I know are no longer connected to the place where they live. They think that tradition is a thing of the past, that it is gone with the wind. People move around frequently these days, looking for better jobs, better school districts and better homes. They trade in houses the way that people in the 'fifties used to trade in cars. Hardly a week goes by in my town during which some new children don't come into school or others leave it. People call this "moving up."

I know professional people who are always talking about their careers. They make deals and are politically astute. They live in a world of negotiations, calculated risks, and gain. That's a game that is hard for anyone to win in the end. For money cannot buy happiness and status will not keep us warm on a cold winter night.

Many of the firefighters at the Falls aren't what you would call "upwardly mobile." Many of them have remained in the Falls much of their lives. Most of them don't want new houses, better school systems, or the vice-presidency of some corporation. They are content to say they are good auto body men or good propane truck drivers and be proud of what they do. They are not driven by the desire for money or power. They never give those things much thought. But they can't drive down the street without waving and they can't go into the Red Mills Market or the

Mahopac National Bank without seeing someone they know and have helped over the years.

Tradition is still alive all over America. You just have to give yourself to it. It will run over you and bathe you like a cleansing rain. It can heal and renew. It connects you to something old and good. It is there waiting.

One day many years from now, in the meeting hall of the Mahopac Falls Volunteer Fire Department, someone will say, "Frank McCluskey has answered his last alarm." The muffled bell will sound and the members will stand in silence. Even if I quit the department this minute, that bell will still be rung. There is a kind of forgiveness there that it took me years to appreciate. No matter what happens in the rest of my life, that is one thing I can count on. It feels good to know that no matter what happens or where I go, when I am gone, the Mahopac Falls Volunteer Fire Department will remember me.

Maybe, a hundred years from now, a new firefighter will walk through the old cemetery behind the Baptist Church looking for a stone with my name on it. He will place a little flag on the grave and linger a minute under a blue May sky. That is the chain of tradition that gathers the generations together and holds us in its arms.

16

Fear, or how to live like there is no tomorrow

There is no fear in love, but perfect love casts out fear.

The Gospel of John

In Zen Buddhism, the whole aim of training is to liberate the mind from fear.

New monks are called "cloud water." This means that they must live every minute like a floating cloud or running water. Any fear or anxiety that might hold them back from living fully must be examined and thrown out. The quest for Zen Enlightenment is a quest to end fear.

It seems to me that many people's problems revolve around some kind of fear. There are as many kinds of fear as there are kinds of people. Each of us has our own demons to face and each of us must walk into that fog that we have created with our own fears and find our way out of it.

Nobody can face our fears for us. We have to do this ourselves. We can put off the moment of truth, but one day we won't
be able to escape it. We're better off if we face our fears sooner
rather than later. Everybody has something they're most afraid
of, and anyone who knows what that fear is knows a great deal
about that person. The writer James Baldwin once said, "Find
what you are afraid of and walk towards it." That simple sentence
is one of most profound and useful statements I have ever read.

When I joined the fire department, I brought some significant
fears with me that would definitely interfere with doing my job as
a firefighter. I've always been afraid of heights and firefighters, of
course, climb on roofs. I've always been claustrophobic, and firefighters have to wear tight masks. I'm not too adept with power
tools and mechanical devices, and firefighters rely on these all
the time. Come to think of it, I probably should have picked
another hobby!

I recall the night that I really licked my fear of heights. For me,
that fear had always been overwhelming. Even re-roofing my little garage was a task. I have a friend, Stan Wiktor, who works as
a Sociology Professor at Mercy College and was once a farmer
in Poland. Although Stan is a professor, his rural roots have given
him a very good understanding of the basic things in life. He
knows how to look problems right in the face and call them what
they are. Stan knows how to repair houses, so he and his friend,
Sasha, came over to help me with my roofing project. The roof
wasn't that far off the ground, but Stan had to literally force me
onto the roof until I was able to bring myself to get the work done
with him. But I was still shaky when the day was over and we'd
completed the task. My fear of heights remained.

The first roof of any significant height that I climbed up on was
during a fire. We had put out a fire on B…. Road and had cut a hole
in or "vent" the roof to let out the smoke and heat. (This lowers the

temperature in the house and makes it safer to fight the fire from inside.) To do this, we use a big power saw with a circular blade that can cut through beams and nails. It's called a K12 and it can be dangerous to use if the roof is steep or the weather conditions are bad.

We had to go up and cover the hole in case it rained that night. Tommy Stasiak pointed to me when the chief told us to get up on the roof. We climbed up on the roof and hoisted ourselves onto a second roof. High in the air, Tommy had me hammering and sawing. My mind was never fully on hammering those nails. I kept glancing down at the ground. I felt the sweat dripping from under my arm and my heart was racing. When the job was complete, I was amazed that I had finished it. The most difficult part, however, was getting down. I was a bit hesitant to back up to the ladder at the edge of the roof. After some coaxing, I did that too, but I didn't like it.

The night that I really licked my fear of heights, though, came when I was again under the watchful eye of Tommy Stasiak. One summer, a few years back, a tornado touched down in the neighboring town of Carmel. We had been out for hours tending to downed wires and trees in the road. Suddenly our tones went off for a rescue truck, power tools, and manpower to respond to an apartment complex near the border between Carmel and Patterson. Walt Swarm got behind the wheel and we loaded up with people. Soon the rescue truck was barreling up Route 6 towards Carmel.

When a mutual-aid call comes from a couple of towns away, we can be sure something major has happened. It means that one town has already had to call the surrounding fire departments before calling on ours. If five or ten departments are already on the scene and more people and equipment are still needed, something has gone very, very wrong.

When we turned down the street next to the scene of the call, we came to a police blockade. Our assistant chief was in the front seat with Walt, as they steered around the blockade into the apartment complex. We were shocked at the destruction that we saw. The tornado had damaged seventy-six houses, some so badly that only a door was left standing. When we arrived, Patterson's new rescue truck was being used to light up one place where it was reported a person was trapped. Later, as we headed north, we heard a call for the county coroner, but fortunately it turned out that no one had died.

We parked our rescue truck in one of the upper lots, turned on our lights, got out our power tools, and started clearing away debris and downed tree limbs. We headed down to the scene of the most wreckage where Tommy Stasiak kept an eye on us as we worked. Carmel had its ladder truck there and people were going up on roofs that had been torn away to put down tarps in case it rained again. They had been up there for a while.

The Carmel firefighters are very friendly with the Falls Firefighters. We have an annual charity basketball game in which we play together against the Carmel police and we play softball against Carmel at least once a year. It's a fun relationship and we know each other well. These sports events and other activities also serve another purpose. If a firefighter is working at an emergency scene with someone they know, things go a lot easier.

The Carmel firefighters had been up on the roofs for two or three hours when Tommy Stasiak decided to ask them if they wanted us to join them up there. "Brilliant idea, Stasiak," I thought to myself. "Send us up on those shaky, broken roofs three stories over a driveway in high winds and see what we can do!" I was all for being helpful, but that offer at that moment seemed beyond my limit.

The Carmel truck drove into place and swiveled the ladder onto a roof. A ladder truck is a amazing piece of equipment to see and even more amazing to be on. The Carmel ladder is eighty-five feet long and was angled up over the parking lot to the top of the townhouses. As the Carmel members came down, Tommy told us we were going up. He and I went to the base of the ladder. Looking up, I could see the long outline of the ladder extending up into the black clouds and the swirling winds; I saw the top of the ladder bouncing in the wind up against the night sky. I was beginning to feel a little on edge. I turned and found myself face to face with Tommy. He was smoking a cigar and looking me dead in the eyes.

Tommy is a serious individual and a formidable one to tangle with. He spends his days confronting convicts and his free time listening to country and western music. If anyone wrongs him, he will let that person know. If anyone gives him a hard time, he will stand up for himself. Tommy believes in the direct approach to life and to people. I often sit in committee meetings with other professors talking very exactly about what we want to do. The talk is slow, careful and polite. Sometime I fantasize that Stasiak walks in and give us his views in no uncertain terms. How that would expedite the process!

Tommy wasn't going to let me get out of this with any false dignity if he could help it. He was going to force me to face my fear.

"You're not scared, are you?"

I gulped. "Me? Whatever gave you that idea?" I turned and climbed up that ladder as fast as I could go. When I got up to the top, I could see that half the roof was gone. The half that remained felt spongy underfoot, like one of those rubber floors in the fun house. The roof seemed unsteady and I was wondering what the heck we were doing up there. Tommy came up the ladder and we started putting down tarp. We took care of that roof and went on and did a few others. As the night wore on, I paid less attention to the height and gave more attention to what I was supposed to be doing. I got used to being up there. Eventually, I was moving around the tower ladder like an old hand. By the time that night was over, my fear of heights was mostly gone. I don't know where it went but I haven't felt it since. One of my psychiatrist friends told me that I had experienced "systematic desensitization." When I told Tommy Stasiak what the psychiatrist had told me, Tommy Stasiak simply said, "Is that what you call it?" He rolled his eyes, shoved the cigar back in his mouth and went back to work.

About a year later, one Friday night in the bar, I told Tommy Stasiak that I had been scared to death the first few times he pushed me up on a roof with him.

"Yeah, I know," he laughed, "I can't stand heights either!"

Tony Luccaro told me about a similar experience he once had. When the old Presbyterian Church caught fire, the whole roof was burning. There was a big bell in the steeple that looked like it might come crashing down. Tony doesn't like heights, but he took the nozzle and charged up a thirty-five foot ladder that was put up against the steeple. He got to the top of the ladder, planning to simply hang on and shoot from the outside. Suddenly there was Walt Swarm, halfway up the ladder with a look of fire in his eyes pointing inside the steeple and yelling, "Get in there!" In the forty-five years he has been in the department, Swarm's enthusiasm has pushed many firefighters into places they hadn't intended to go. Tony got off the ladder (very carefully, as he tells it) and got inside the steeple where the fire was blazing. Since that time, Tony has been more careful about preceding Swarm up a ladder.

Perhaps my biggest test came recently when we got a call for a structure fire. I was riding in the cab of our first attack truck next to Walt Swarm when I looked at the direction we were headed and saw a column of black smoke rising in the air. I gulped. Even dispatcher Mike Johnson sounded just the slightest bit excited.

"Carmel Police to all Mahopac Falls home fire monitors. We have a confirmed, fully-involved working structure fire on S.... road."

I picked up the radio microphone to tell the County Sheriff's Department that we were responding. "19-2-3 to 40 Control"

"Go ahead, 19-2-3." (They had gotten our transmission.)

"Mahopac Falls 19-2-3, 19-4-2, 19-6-1, and 19-7-1 responding to a structure fire on S.... Road."

This told them our engine, rescue truck, and ambulance were on the way. We hit Route 6N flying and made time going up the hill past the Presbyterian Church. The siren was blasting and I was finishing buttoning my coat and strapping on my bottle as we flew.

I looked in the rearview mirror and saw all the big trucks with their sirens and lights going roaring and screaming their way toward the fire. Suddenly, the tones went off again. They were calling for everything. It was a "worker" and it looked like I was going to be the first officer on the scene. I started trying to think through all of the possibilities we might encounter.

We turned up the street and saw the fire raging. It had come through the roof and the whole back of the house was on fire. The flames were fifty feet in the air. The driveway was all ice. Walt stopped at the bottom only long enough for me to pull off the supply line. When he drove up the driveway, he would leave a trail of hose behind. This is called "laying line." It lets us supply water to the attack truck with tankers from the road instead of having to go up the driveway. I was out of the cab and running to the house. When I got there, I found Tommy Stasiak setting up a hose line in the back. I got some of the rookies to get the ladders and start pulling the line.

There were dozens of things to do and many of them weren't getting done. Tommy Stasiak and some of the others had taken an inch-and-a-half line and gone to the door. Tommy kicked it down, while the others put on their air bottles, then they started inside. Smoke was coming out of every crack in the house. The fire was crackling and snapping.

At that moment, the captain looked over and pointed to me. "Lieutenant, get in there with those men and make sure they're okay!"

I ran up onto the porch and felt the heat. I got in the door and felt even more heat pouring out. I knew Tommy and the others were already inside, so I pulled my visor down, and grabbed the hose line. I followed that line into the blackness, looking for my friends. Just on the other side of the door I saw them. They were spraying a fog mist on a fireball the size of a Mack truck. Tommy pushed his mask toward me and yelled, "It feels like we're in some kind of hallway. One of the guys thinks there are stairs there but we can't see."

All that I remembered at that moment were the stories I had heard about Swarm when he was a young lieutenant. I thought about what he would say at this moment. I got behind the others and yelled, "Get in there!" Then I tried to duck behind Stasiak in case it got too hot.

In the darkness and smoke, there was a good deal of confusion as we tried to move ahead. There was an obstacle in our way (it turned out to be a large exercise bike) and we tried unsuccessfully to move it. We had a difficult time getting around it. We couldn't see. Tommy hit the wall and lost his helmet but kept fighting the fire. I sent him outside to get another one. One of the other firefighters had been in such a rush to get inside he had forgotten his gloves. I never finished buttoning my coat and

Tommy Stasiak was still wearing his work clothes under his fire-fighting gear.

As the battle raged inside, I backed out to see how the operations were going outside the house. I walked back out onto the porch and called the captain on my portable radio. He told me to ventilate the fire by opening the windows in the house. I tried to open the windows, but they had been sealed shut. All of the metal and wood had expanded in the heat and would not move. It was so hot that a gas grill on the back porch had melted and fallen over and what was once a television set was just a gray puddle. I took an axe and began to smash the windows that were in the current path of the fire, providing ventilation so that it wouldn't change direction and turn on us.

The firefighters continued to put water on the fire and move it back. They kept pushing it until eventually they began to run out of air. All three of them had taken turns on the nozzle fighting the fire. The heat was so brutal we could not stay in the fire for long. Teams shuffled in and out spelling each other. The heat, the smoke, and the power of a fire sap every bit of strength and resolve you have. It dehydrates you and steals all of your vitamins, minerals, salts and energy. If you battle long enough, it can steal your heart. But eventually the black smoke pouring out of the windows began to turn to gray. This meant that the fire was being turned to steam and we were winning the war. It is a color that firefighters love.

After the fire was knocked down, Tommy and I went outside for a break. Exhausted, dirty, and smelling of smoke, we still had several hours of salvage, overhaul and fire quenching to do. I imagined that we would sleep well that night. We had done a good day's work for the community.

Later, back at the firehouse, the gear was being washed, the hoses were being cleaned, and the sodas were being consumed in large numbers. The radio was on as always. It was tuned to WHUD and the Classics Four were singing *Stormy.*

But I still had one more lesson to learn about fear. That night, I woke up with a start around 3:00 a.m. I was sweating. In some dream world the fire had gotten behind us and I couldn't find my way out of that dark, flaming hall. I felt my heart race for a few minutes. I was still dealing with the terror of being in that night's fire. After my efforts during the day, the fear had retreated to another place inside of me. Many of those feelings now live only in my nightmares. The more we confront frightening things when we're awake, the more solid we become as human beings. Fear is something we have to face eventually. We can't run away, even in our dreams.

When I lay back down to go to sleep, I wondered what the Falls firefighters were afraid of. I had been standing behind three of them in a house on fire a few hours earlier and I think that the answer is—they aren't afraid of too much.

Many of our problems come from fear—fear of love, fear of success, fear of failure, fear of taking a chance. But the firefighters I work with live like they're not afraid. Without fear in their waking life, they can live with a kind of poise and grace, with what a friend of mine calls "quiet dignity." Fear exists only if we let it. I think of my fear of heights as an example. If only I had been introduced to Tommy Stasiak when I was sixteen, think of all of the money I could have saved on roofers.

17

Perfection, or how to live with mistakes

Perfection is a trifle dull. It is not the least of life's ironies that this, which we all aim at, is better not quite achieved.

W. Somerset Maugham

The desire for perfection is one of the worst ideas anyone could have. It can be like a caustic acid that can destroy anything it comes into contact with. It can ruin your relationships, estrange you from your children and bring unhappiness to your work. Give up the idea of perfection my friends; it exists only in our minds. Some of the great philosophers, even people like Plato, were not immune to this disease. They imagined a realm of perfect forms that we should copy. Wrong, because once we have the idea there is such a thing as a perfect world, this world, the real world, ceases to shine.

One problem with this approach is that it sets up an ideal of perfection that doesn't really exist. The whole concept of perfection bothers me. It's a goal or idea that can have a negative impact on a person's whole life if they're not careful. For instance, some of the more intelligent youngsters that I knew when I was in school thought that being smart meant they had to be perfect. To me, that is the worst way to look at the joys of school. I used to know a girl who was a straight-A student all throughout high school. When she got to college and she got a B-plus, it was a traumatic experience for her. Trying to do one's best is great; however, we are going too far when trying to be perfect makes us unhappy.

One of the worst ideas people could have is that they have to be perfect. Some people think that being perfect is their duty. They think that they should have a perfect marriage, perfect children, and perfect homes all the time.

Well, we all know how things really work out in life. Our marriages aren't perfect, our houses aren't perfect and, heaven knows, our children aren't perfect. Then what happens to perfectionists? First, they get frustrated because they fail to reach their goals; next, they get angry; and then they get depressed. If they're not perfect and they think they should be, they see themselves as failures. They've set up their lives as a game where they're trapped. Once they define the alternatives as perfection or failure, they can't win. If they can't win, they can't be happy. The perfection game is a losing game. I've never known anybody who can beat the odds.

That doesn't mean we can't be excellent in what we do. By excellence, I mean being the best that we can be at any given time. A teacher should try to be the best teacher he can be; a butcher should try to be the best butcher in town; a painter should try to paint houses to the best of her ability. Martin Luther

King once said to a street sweeper that he should "sweep the streets like Michelangelo painted paintings."

Our own lives should be a work of art.

There is a fellow in our fire department named Gary Link who fixes cars in his spare time and stands as a model of excellence to me. He is the best mechanic we have. He does good work and charges a fair price. If, now and again, he fixes something and it doesn't stay fixed, he will take care of the problem free of charge. He may not be perfect but he is the closest thing to it. He never gets bent out of shape and always does what he has promised to do. with his whole heart, he gives it his all. He knows the secret of achieving excellence: doing your best and being wise enough to know when you've reached your limits.

Whenever things go wrong, whether I forget something important or just forget to pick up a carton of milk at the Red Mills Market, I try to remember that nobody's perfect. Nothing human can be without fault. This cliché is the most profound truth in the universe. The Bible tells us that after Adam and Eve were kicked out of Paradise they had to live with their faults and imperfections. We're their children, so we've got these imperfections too. But once we realize that nobody's perfect, and let that truth sink into our behavior and attitudes, we can relax a bit and see life in a clearer light. If more people would learn not to expect perfection, they could be much happier.

At my last high school reunion, I spent time with the guys on my old football team. I was a mediocre player and as a team we didn't always play up to our potential. But we had one or two moments in the sun that I'll remember into my next life. We didn't have any perfect seasons, but we had some perfect moments. When I went to the reunion, I met our old fullback, who went on to attend Princeton and then become an executive at one of the biggest stock brokerage houses in New York City. Instead of talking about his success or his money, he reminded me of a big play that had involved both of us twenty years before. That memory was more important to him than bragging about any of his accomplishments. He had been the All-State fullback, and he could have reminded me of that, but he was kind enough not to do so. Instead, he reminded me of one shining moment I had had carrying the football, a moment I hadn't thought about myself in twenty years. When I reminisced about those days, I was often haunted by the missed chances and the times our team had come up short. He remembered a moment on a beautiful autumn day, a long time ago, when I had broken into the open field with the ball tucked under my arm. I can remember breaking the tackle, reversing direction and getting into a full gallop with the other team in pursuit. All of the colors and scents came back to me. He awoke a memory in me that had been sleeping for twenty years. I remembered a slow-motion view of the open field as I picked up speed, the sight of the stands full of my schoolmates out of the corner of my eye, and the bright red and orange leaves behind them. Those were good days. We did our best and once in a while we did the impossible, like the time our hopelessly outmatched team had beaten the most powerful team in our conference. We weren't perfect, maybe not even excellent, but we were okay. Once we know the world isn't perfect, we are free to be ourselves a little more.

In the 'sixties there was a book called *I'm OK, You're OK*. The idea in this book is that everyone deserves to feel good. Sometime later I got my hands on a tee shirt that took that title a little further. It said, "I'm not OK, You're not OK, but that's OK" I liked that. Nobody's perfect, but everybody counts. And every minute counts. Once it's gone, it won't come again. Today will soon be gone and we should savor every taste, every color, every sound.

I've heard people talk about moving away from Mahopac Falls and going someplace "better." I learned long ago, however, that "better" and "worse" aren't places in the world, only ideas in people's heads. Those words are no more real than Plato's forms. The world isn't perfect, but for me, Mahopac Falls is perfect in its own way.

A firefighter also has to learn to deal with imperfection because we're human, too, and we make mistakes. On every serious fire or ambulance call, many things are happening very quickly. Some details get overlooked and some things get forgotten. Whenever we have a bad call—one where something has gone wrong—we go back to the firehouse and do a critique. We sit around and talk about the call. We talk about how we could have solved the same problems differently and what we should remember the next time. Some of the best critics in these exercises are our chiefs. They raise hard questions and try to go over every detail. They talk about what we did right and what we did wrong. They know we're in a business where mistakes can be costly. Lately, I've taken over doing the critiques. We pull out a blackboard and the chiefs talk about problems such as where the hose lines were, what challenges we had getting water to the fire quickly, how we directed the path of the fire, and how effectively we communicated. I am a little more laid back than some of the other officers. They are more direct about letting someone know when he or she should be moving faster, making different decisions, or following through on certain procedures. We talk about how we can pull the hose quicker. We talk about what cost us time. We try to improve how we do things. Sometimes we praise and other times we tell our members we have to do better. That's what an officer is supposed to do.

Have you ever seen a fire truck go flying by with the lights flashing and the siren screeching? Do you always assume, as I used to, that the crew actually knows where they're going? Well, when I joined the Falls, I found out it's not always true. Even though we try our best to eliminate them, sometimes we make some big mistakes.

One case in point that I remember involved a brush fire that we had one night a few summers back. A brush fire is a fire in the woods and it's not usually as dangerous as a structure fire. The call came in on a Friday night and the firefighters went running to the trucks. They do this for two reasons. First, as I'm sure you understand by now, in a fire, every second can count. Second—let's be honest here—many people want to drive a truck at high speed on an emergency run, ignoring most of the traffic regulations. That's a pleasure not everyone can have—at least not legally.

On this particular night there was the usual scramble to the trucks. The first attack truck got out fast and was gone before anyone else got down to the engine room floor. Some of the people who were left headed to the brush truck, which is equipped with tools needed to fight a brush fire. It carries rakes, shovels, and chain saws, along with tanks of water for us to carry on our backs into the woods. Two of our younger (and less experienced) members jumped into the brush truck and shot off. I was up in the radio room with some of the old-timers who were manning the radio. The radio room is on the second floor of the fire station and has big windows with a good view of the parking lot and the road. We saw the brush truck race up to the flashing light where the road we're on joins 6N and take a right onto it and speed away. We were all quiet for a little while.

"Guys" I started, "weren't they supposed to turn left?"

Art Brady expresses himself carefully. "I was wondering the same thing myself," he said.

"They must know where they're going. They wouldn't just take a truck and head off without knowing where the call is."

Well, it turns out that was just what they had done. After another minute, the attack pumper called in. They were at the scene fighting a fairly big brush fire. Walt Swarm radioed back to the base and asked, "Where's the brush truck?"

At this point we called the brush truck. "19-3-1, where are you?"

"We're going down Hill Street."

We now realized what was happening. Our radio dispatcher, a seasoned veteran with thirty years in the department, smiled as he asked the brush truck crew to switch to channel two. That's the channel on our pager that we use when there's something embarrassing to say.

"19-3-1, turn around at Bullet Hole Road, the fire is on the other side of the district on Wood Street. You're going the wrong way!"

The truck took the next turn-around and headed back. The saga, however, wasn't over. About ten minutes later, the attack pumper was in the woods fighting the fire when the crew saw the brush truck coming. Imagine their surprise when the brush truck sped past them and continued, lights and sirens blasting, on its way to who knows where.

Walt Swarm called in. He was getting excited by this time. He was going to kill whoever was in that truck. How could they start out not knowing where the fire was and then turn around and drive right past it? He called in on channel one, "Where the hell are they?"

Suddenly the brush truck came back on the air. One of the young guys was on the radio. "This is 19-3-1. What was the location of that fire again?"

At this point, someone in the radio room expressed our amazement by paraphrasing the opening words of *Star Trek*: "They've boldly gone where no man has gone before."

Not only are regular firefighters not perfect, even chiefs have been known to have a bad day—at least that happened to our Assistant chief, Mike Dadabo.

About every hundred years in Mahopac Falls, we get more rains than the drains can handle. The last time that happened was in the first decade of this century, and it happened again one summer a few years ago. It had been raining for days and the ground was already soaked. There was no place left for the water to go. Suddenly, we got ten inches of rain in one day. Calls started to pour in for the fire department to come and pump out people's basements. A good number of the other rural fire departments don't do "pump-outs" because it is too costly and time-consuming. That's another way that the Falls is kind of special. If one of our neighbors calls and needs his or her basement pumped, we wouldn't feel neighborly if we didn't lend a hand.

One of the calls on that rainy day was to Assistant Chief Mike Dadabo's house in Lake Secor. Mike, who is a Vietnam veteran, delivers mail in a nearby town. He has a hands-on style and is always on top of the situation. He called because he was getting a good deal of water flooding into the basement. With most of the regular drivers out at other pump-outs all over town, two firefighters (who will remain nameless) jumped into one of our big tankers and started it up. The chief was at the firehouse and noticed these two fellows didn't have much experience operating the big trucks.

"Are you two sure you know how to pump this thing?"

The two smiled with the misplaced confidence that is frequently present at the beginning of misadventures. "Don't worry, Chief, we've got it."

Well they drove our Mack 10-wheel tanker carrying 2,000 gallons of water over to Mike Dadabo's house. It was his daughter's eighteenth birthday, and with his basement three inches deep in water, he was in a rather ornery mood. The truck arrived and parked in Mike's driveway, which angled down toward his garage. It was pouring rain. Not being regular truck operators, the fire-fighters forgot to put chocks under the wheels, so when they put the truck into pump gear, the gear popped out and the big truck started to roll slowly toward Mike's little house. Mike loves his house and did what any normal, rational homeowner would do if a Mack truck started to roll toward it: he put his hands on the bumper and tried to push it back up.

Naturally, in that tug-of-war between Mike and the Mack, Mike lost. The truck rolled down the driveway, Mike jumped out of the way, and the truck crashed into the side of his house with such force that it knocked the house off its foundation. The birthday party was ruined and the basement was flooded. Everything in two bedrooms and the garage was a total loss. The house had been knocked off its foundation by a truck from Mike's own department, while he, an assistant chief, stood there and watched.

But worse things were coming for Mike that day.

Mike was so depressed about these two disasters that he decided to get his mind off his own problems. He went out with the various pump-out crews to make sure everything was all right in other places. There were seventy-two requests for pump-outs that day. Every truck was out and we worked in the pouring rain until dawn. By ten o'clock that night, we were soaked and exhausted. We had been out in cold rain for hours, lifting pumps and hose and crawling inside people's basements. Later than night, we finished a pump-out and I got into the chief's car with Mike to go to the next call where a crew was waiting. We never got there.

In the midst of all of the rain and confusion, we met, in the mid-dle of the road, another vehicle that wouldn't move toward the side in response to the flashing red light that Mike had on his dashboard. Mike honked his siren. Nothing happened. Mike exchanged some angry words with the other driver. Then Mike did what any good ex-Marine in his forties would do under the circumstances—he jumped out of the car and got into a fight with three teenagers. (My own part in this ugly affair is still a matter of debate in the department. I say that I got thrown against the car and broke my finger. Mike's version is that I, like a good professor, got on the roof and limited my help to yelling, "Watch it, Mike; here comes another one!") Anyway, the police showed up and hauled us all into the police station on assault charges. That day with Mike Dadabo was far from perfect but it surely was memorable.

I recall reading a book of Chinese philosophy that said, "No flower is perfect, but each flower is perfect." On the surface, this statement sounds like a contradiction. If you spend a little time with it, you will begin to see the deeper meaning. To me, it means that everything and every situation have their own qualities and special merits. Nothing works without a hitch in this life. Things go wrong, things don't work, and our feelings sometime take a beating. Still, everything needs to be accepted for what it is, not for some abstract idea of what it should be.

I sometimes remember my high school football team. We won some and lost some. We had as many lows as we had highs. But I sometimes, especially since that conversation at the reunion, catch a glimpse of those gold helmets gleaming in the sun, the band playing off-key, and my girlfriend, in the color guard; smiling a smile I haven't seen in thirty years. I can still hear the Turtles singing *Happy Together*.

Somehow, it seems perfect now and, in its own way, I guess it was then, too.

No, we aren't perfect down at the Falls firehouse. Yes, one day the brush truck missed a fire completely, and another day, a truck crashed into Mike Dadabo's house. Day in and day out, however, we do more right than we do wrong. When there's a fire in the Falls in the next year or two, Mike Dadabo and those firefighters on that brush truck will show up and make a difference. They may not be perfect, but if I jump off a truck and see Mike Dadabo in charge, I know we'll all be okay. That's about as close to perfect as I need to be.

18

Swans, or appreciating every living thing

On the score of foreknowledge and divination I am infinitely inferior to the swans. When they perceive the approach of death, they sing more beautifully than before, because of the joy they have of going to the god they serve.

Plato

Legend has it that Socrates and his most famous pupil, Plato, both had dreams involving swans. The night before he first met Plato, Socrates dreamed of a swan that sang a beautiful melodic song. The next day he met Plato, who wrote the most beautiful prose in praise of philosophy. The second swan dream was Plato's. The night before he died, he dreamed there was a swan that the hunters could not catch. It flew from tree to tree and escaped their nets. Perhaps that swan represents the meaning of Plato's dialogues, which are still debated by scholars today. We have yet to capture the swan.

There are many folktales, myths, and legends about animals. Many stories throughout the history of literature involve birds and animals. Melville's whale, Poe's raven, and Blake's tiger are all famous. These fictional creatures stand for that other side of human nature. That side of us is more innocent, more primitive, and more honest. We sometimes lose touch with that part of ourselves. To quote the poet Wallace Stevens, "The bird sings a foreign song." That bird is our other side, that side of us that speaks without words. It is the part of ourselves that is so in touch with things that there are no words that can match the experience. Words can sometimes dull our experience. Once we have a word or concept for something, we cease to think about it and to look at it critically. But when there are no words for something it appears new and mysterious. I have often thought that this is the way that animals must see the world. Every now and then, we can look at the world without the aid of words. When we are in this state we are like a tiger that walks by rivers that have no name and who lives in a world without words, without explanations and without excuses.

The Falls has more animal stories than can be told in any book. There are stories, for example, about dogs, cats, bats, deer, and even some swans. One dog story happened just recently on New Year's Eve. There was a New Year's Eve party in progress at the firehouse, so we were all there. About eight o'clock at night, a call came in that a dog had gotten its paw stuck in a tree and couldn't get it out. Walt Swarm and Tommy Stasiak headed out with the rescue truck to extricate Fido. They got to the house, and sure enough, there was a dog with its paw stuck. It had tried to jump a fence, its paw had gotten stuck in a hole in a tree and the paw was now wedged in there very tightly.

Walt and Tommy used what we call the Jaws of Life to spread the tree. The dog was yowling, the owners were excited, our members made their usual witty repartee, but eventually the dog got its paw free and was okay.

When Walt and Tommy got back to the New Year's Eve party at the firehouse, I asked Stasiak if the dog had licked them in appreciation.

"Licked us? The damn thing tried to bite us!"

The type of dog usually associated with firehouses is the Dalmatian. There's a history behind this. Back in the 1700's, Dalmatians were used as "coach dogs." When the stagecoaches rode through towns, the Dalmatians would run ahead and clear the way so that the horses wouldn't get spooked. Before then, fire departments had engines that were hand-pulled. (Our neighboring department Carmel still has one of these. They've nicknamed it the "Old Buckeye," and it sits in their station by Lake Glenida.) When the fire departments changed from hand-pulled steam engines to horse-drawn ones, they knew Dalmatians calmed down horses, so they used them with their new engines. The dogs have been around firehouses ever since.

Mahopac Falls had a Dalmatian for a few weeks some years ago. One of our more active members bought a cute little Dalmatian puppy he named "Smokey." Smokey was an energetic little puppy and would prance around the fire department, always wanting to play. When it came time for the big Memorial Day parade in Mahopac, we were going to let Smokey ride in the passenger's seat of the Little Mack. Well, Smokey was in the passenger seat of the 1939 Little Mack and just as the parade began, he fell asleep. Walt Swarm, who was driving, tried to wake him up but to no avail. The dog snored all the way through the parade down Main Street and didn't wake up until the trucks had turned down East Lake Boulevard. In time, we discovered that Smokey had a few other bad habits that I will not mention here, which cost him his job as the official mascot of the Falls. He still comes around, but when he visits, we try to keep him away from the trucks.

We've also had some dealings with bats. The old firehouse was in a converted one-room school building with a bell tower, just the sort of place that bats like to inhabit, and the Falls bell tower had become the home to literally hundreds of bats. The bats didn't seem to bother anybody, and since firefighters are generally a "live and let live" kind of group, they just left them there. In fact, some of our old-time members who were enthusiastic gardeners used to go up into the steeple to get bat droppings, which they swore by, for their organic gardens. The gardeners used to bring around good-sized tomatoes in August, but after we found out what had been used for fertilizer, some of the firefighters not would touch them.

When the town built a new station, the old one, along with the bell tower, was torn down. This meant that the bats lost their home. After that, they started nesting in the attics and eaves of every house, barn, and garage in Mahopac Falls. Complaint after complaint came into the firehouse. One of the people across the street even got a lawyer and was going to sue the Department. But when our lawyer told his lawyer that the town couldn't be held responsible for non-domesticated animals; that was the end of the dispute. After all, the fire department didn't own the bats.

The bat problem didn't end there, however. The bats continued to be a nuisance, pulling the siding off one house, making their home in local attics, frightening people with their sudden, darting movements, and even driving several people out of their homes. Eventually, the town called a forest ranger at Carlesbad Caverns, long distance, to find out if there was anything we could do. The bats eventually relocated but the firefighters weren't too popular with the locals for a couple of months.

There are many deer in my town. You don't have to walk very far to spot them. A few winters ago, our tones went off on a Saturday afternoon. I had a house full of company, but I listened any way.

"Carmel Police to all Mahopac Falls home rescue monitors. Assistance is needed for a deer that has fallen through the ice by Interlocken in Kirk Lake."

I said goodbye to my friends, hopped into my car and sped off to the firehouse. Walt Jackel and Tony Luccaro are members of the Scuba Rescue Team at the Falls. They got the metal boat and oars, and we pulled out of the station. As we headed toward Kirk Lake, Tony looked around with a wild expression.

"Any suggestions about what we do when we get there?" he asked me half jokingly.

The truck pulled up and we hiked about a half-mile through the woods to get to the shoreline. I looked out toward the middle of the lake and saw a big buck with its front hooves on the ice and its lower body in the water. It was about a hundred feet from shore and was still alive. When we got there, I stepped onto the ice and heard it crack and groan. I stepped back. Our members were bringing down the poles, ropes, and boat. Tony and Walt Jackel were putting on life jackets. Walt had worked for ConEd Power Company for thirty years. He still sports a haircut that Elvis would be proud of. Walt is never without a gold chain on which is a navy anchor to remind him of his service to his country.

The two of them got into the boat and started to push themselves off onto the ice. We tied a rope to the stern of the boat just in case they got into trouble. Before he shoved off, Tony took me aside and said, "If anything happens to us out there, don't take too many chances yourself—that water is cold." I appreciated what Tony was telling me, and I just smiled; I knew he was more than a little nervous. He had never tried to rescue a wild animal from an icy lake before. To be perfectly honest, none of us had even heard of this being done before!

Tony and Walt pushed off. Those of us on the shore, all wearing life jackets, watched as the boat skimmed slowly across the ice toward the stranded deer. It seemed like an eternity passed as they moved along the white surface toward the middle. The boat skidded slowly across the top of the ice as they used their paddles to move forward.

By now a crowd had gathered, including some reporters from the local papers. I tried to keep the crowd away from the shore in case we had to act fast. The deer was a large and powerful creature. Anything could happen. If they got the deer and it started to thrash, the boat could tip over. They were a long way from the shore. The deer also had a huge rack of sharp antlers. We all had our fingers crossed on this one.

Tony and Walt Jackel were finally close to the deer. Tony went to the bow of the boat and tried to get hold of the animal's shoulders. The buck flailed wildly and almost tossed Tony out of the boat. Walt signaled for us to pull on the safety rope and we quickly pulled the boat away from the thrashing animal. Tony and Walt were talking to each other. We didn't know what they were saying, and I was wondering if they were going to ask us to pull them back in and just go home. But they aren't the quitting type. They fashioned a loop out of one of the ropes and prepared to try to lasso the deer. Firefighters are expected to learn all sorts of knots when they first join. I was taught ten or fifteen, and I remember some of their names like the "chimney hitch" or the "sheep shank," but I can never keep them straight. Fortunately, Walt Jackel remembered.

Walt took out the oar and pushed the boat closer to the big buck. Tony stood up and threw his rope at the deer. He missed. He tried again and missed a second time. On about the fifth attempt, Tony got the rope around the deer's neck and it slid down around its shoulder. The rope was on. Walt signaled for us to start pulling slowly. We started to pull gently on the rope and bring the boat back toward shore. When the boat moved, the rope tightened around the deer's neck and the boat came to a halt. Tony signaled us to stop pulling.

Walt tugged gently on the rope and pulled the deer up out of the hole in the ice. The deer managed to stand up, but then it slid back down again. We started pulling the boat back along toward the shore while the deer still struggled wildly. It was shaking its head and yanking on the rope. It pulled and thrashed with all of the strength it had left. It seemed, several times, that the boat and the deer would tip over out on that thin ice. In the stillness of the winter air, you could hear the ice cracking and moaning beneath the struggle. Tony had a determined look on his face as we pulled as quickly as we could. We had never done anything like this before and none of us knew how it was going to turn out.

We were pulling desperately when suddenly something happened that none of us had expected. The deer collapsed about fifty feet from shore. We pulled the boat back in and went out onto the ice to get the deer. We used caution approaching the large animal. It had lost consciousness, but it could wake up at any minute. We lifted the deer and carried it off the ice and into the surrounding woods. We began to massage and rub the deer gently. One of the guys went to the rescue truck and got a blanket. We put the blanket over the deer and continued to massage it. It's skin felt like a cowhide coat that you might find in the old West. It was cool to the touch and rough. The deer had a sweet smell of the woods about it. It was breathing deeply but was still unconscious. It had gotten quite a shock to its system.

I was up by the head of the deer when it suddenly opened its eyes. I don't know how aware it was, but it looked at me with big brown eyes. A number of the people around us backed up but I didn't move. It was not out of any sense of courage. It was just that I was so amazed that the whole scenario was unfolding as it was. A deer is a huge animal and if it jumped up, it could hurt me, but it seemed strangely at peace and I felt at peace, too. Few people have had the privilege to hold a live wild deer in their arms. Not everybody has been eye to eye that close with a live buck. I petted its nose and moved away. The deer tried to get up, took a few steps, and fell down, but it had taken three steps.

Walt Jackel told us to step back and leave the deer alone. We took all of the equipment back to the truck. The crowd had dispersed and the police were keeping people from the woods. We took the truck back to the Falls, washed it down, and refitted all of our equipment. Reporters from the local papers were interviewing Tony and Walt We were all frozen. Somebody upstairs had made some hot soup and coffee and it tasted delicious.

We had been out on the icy lake for more than an hour but I was more curious about the deer than I was hungry. I got into my car and headed back to Kirk Lake. I drove down Interlocken and parked my car. The blanket we had left on the deer was hanging on a tree branch about two hundred feet from the shore. There were hoof marks heading along the bank and off into the woods. Our friend had gone and a warm feeling went through me.

This rescue was a big story in the local papers. We even got mentioned on the country and western station that broadcasts out of New York City. Tony and Walt Jackel were local celebrities for a few weeks after that. They even got invited to the annual dinner of an animal lover's society down county and were given an award.

Now, rescuing cats is a different matter. In fact, for a while, the department didn't rescue cats in trees because the firefighters almost always got clawed and the cats would then run down the tree anyway. As Tommy Stasiak once said to me, "Think of it, pal, has anybody ever seen a cat skeleton in a tree? No, never, and I'll tell you why, pal. When they get hungry they get down. But firefighters haven't figured this out in three hundred years!"

Jack Casey likes to tell a story about a cat that got caught in a tree down in Lake Baldwin. One day a call came in from a woman who sounded distraught. She told the firefighters that her cat was stuck thirty feet up in a tree and she wanted them to come and rescue it. We'd recently had some bad incidents involving cats stuck in trees. We would climb up but almost always get the bad end of the deal. Being thirty feet up the air in a tree is a feat in itself. It is another thing to do that while a cat is trying to scratch your eyes out. We told the woman that the Falls fire department wasn't interested in getting her cat out of a tree. She sounded disappointed and hung up. About thirty minutes later, the same woman called back.

"Could you please come quick to my house for a tree rescue? Come quickly!"

Jack Casey took the call and remembers it well. "Lady, didn't you just call us a little while ago? I told you we don't rescue cats!"

"Cats!" she screamed. "Forget the cats! My husband went up to get the poor thing and now they're both up there! Come quick!"

The firefighters arrived and put up a thirty-five foot ladder. They helped get the husband down, but he wasn't pleased with his wife for having him climb the tree in the first place. They also rescued the cat. And yes, she scratched the dickens out of the firefighter who was trying to save her.

Feelings for animals, including cats, still run deep for many of us. There was an incident some time back in my town where a family lost everything they owned in a bad fire, including their little kitten, that didn't make it out of the smoke and flames. After the fire, the chief sent Jack Casey and me into the basement to make sure that no fire was smoldering. Jack and I started to take things away from the walls. Everything was wrapped neatly in newspapers and bags, so we didn't know what we were moving.

While we were working, I asked Jack if he was okay. Jack is one of the kindest and most sensitive people I've ever met. He smiled sadly.

"I got their kitty out of there and buried it. I didn't want the kids to go back in there and find it. You know, it always breaks my heart when I see that."

I have a special love for furry little things myself and I sympathized with Jack's view of animals. We had been through a lot that afternoon and to show Jack that I felt the way he did, I shared something as personal with him as he had just shared with me.

"You know, Jack, my mother named me "Francis" after Saint Francis of Assisi. It was said he loved the animals and he even once spoke to a wolf that was terrorizing a village and made the wolf repent. There is a statue of him holding his hand out with a little bird in it. They say sparrows would land in his hand whenever he held it out. I like being named after someone like that."

At that very moment, Jack pulled out the next wad of newspapers. He carefully peeled them away and there in his hands was a porcelain statue of Saint Francis of Assisi, holding a little sparrow in his outstretched hand.

Just the other Sunday morning, we were down at the Falls firehouse tending our trucks. My son, Brandon, was with me, and I was showing him how to check the oil and bleed the air out of the brakes on the old rescue truck. We were drinking coffee and chatting. The radio was tuned to WHUD as usual and the Beatles were singing *She loves you.*

Around nine a.m., a call came in to the Carmel police that some swans were stuck in the ice over on Lake Secor. Camille Lapine, Tommy Stasiak, and Tony Luccaro got into the brush truck and headed over there. Brandon and I followed in my car. Stasiak grumbled, "I've lived here all of my life, and this is the first time I ever heard of swans getting stuck in the ice! You're going to risk your lives for birds like that? Hell, they might be too dumb to live!" Tommy may have had a point with his Darwinian view of things, but off we went. It might have been risky to rescue swans from the ice. But these weren't just any living things; they were swans. I remembered my Plato, and I would have chanced it.

We drove out into the winter morning and eventually arrived at the spot. It turned out that the call was not needed. The swans had freed themselves from the ice and were gliding majestically on the water. As we stood there on the bank, I realized for the first time that, like every other creature, swans didn't need to find a path, because with every turn they make in water, they create their own path. Sailing through water is like flying, or floating on air: there is no right or wrong turn in the air or on the water.

Buddhists believe that, like humans, animals are life forms on a journey. Each one is sacred. Each one is special. Like followers of the majority of the world's religions, Buddhists believe in reincarnation. The Greek philosopher, Pythagoras, whose views echoed eastern religions, believed that sometimes the souls of humans pass after death into the souls of animals. In his dialogue *Phaedo*, Plato tells us that good citizens might be reborn as ants or bees, while others are reborn as wolves or donkeys. The energy that inhabits us doesn't die. It only changes form, likes waves on the ocean. As I watched the swans swimming gracefully, I thought of this. Perhaps there floating on the water were Socrates and Plato dreaming different dreams.

19

Light, or how to step out of the darkness

Not every light is a true light. To the wise the light of truth is light itself.

Tiruvalluvar

Every one of us has spent time looking for the light. We have all spent time lost in dark labyrinths looking for that golden thread that could be our way out. Sometimes, it seems that the light is gone for good. In this world where there is so much corruption and ignorance, it is hard for many people to believe there is a light at the end of the tunnel, but I think there is.

In the Far East there are people who think the whole aim of life is to find the light. People who have found it are called "enlightened." A Guru once told me it takes 10,000 reincarnations and 10,000 lifetimes to become enlightened. The lesson to be learned in all of these lifetimes is not really complicated.

When firefighters go into a burning building, the smoke is sometimes so dark and thick that they can't see anything. They feel their way with their hands, groping in the dark to find the right way. As they go in, they are looking for fire. Fire is the beacon that lights their path. It is also a beacon that warns them away. They move blindly through the black of the smoke searching for the light, searching for the source. They can only stay in a fire as long as their air bottles hold out. Air packs contain an alarm that sounds a muffled rattle in the mask. When firefighters hear that alarm, they have five minutes to get outside before they run out of air. One breath of toxic smoke and super-heated air could coat their lungs and kill them. When that alarm goes off, they have to turn away from the light and plunge back into the darkness, feeling the hose line, trying to find their way back out. They have to trust themselves, their air packs and their friends. They have to trust each of them with their lives.

Sometimes in the darkness, heat, and confusion, firefighters cannot find the way out. Some have not made it out at all. This is always in the back of many firefighters minds when they are in the darkness and the light is nowhere to be seen. Tommy Stasiak has been in as many fires as anybody I know. He knows how confusing it can be. He says that in a fire, you can be in a ten-foot by 10-foot room but you think you're lost in Yankee Stadium. You can get an idea of what this is like by trying a simple exercise. Have someone put a blindfold on you and then spin you around and lead you to some part of the house that is unfamiliar to you. Then get down on all fours and see how difficult it is to find your way. That is what we do in every fire we go into.

Sometimes it feels like we will never find the way out. We wonder if we're going in a direction that is leading us deeper into somewhere we should not be—away from the light.

Light is not just something found in fires. It is said to be the goal of the soul after the darkness of death. In my experience with the ambulance, I have had a chance to talk with members of other ambulance corps who have been involved in some cases of near-death experiences. This is when a patient has no pulse or respiration and later comes back to consciousness. Many of these people talk about the incredible visions that they had while they were "dead." One woman told me that she saw a light and that she wanted to go toward it but a voice told her to wait. It was not her time to move on. It was not yet time to go into the light.

I have not been in as many fires as some other people I know, but the ones I've been in are still as clear as daylight to me. Fires are such powerful memories that an old firefighter like Walt Swarm can tell you blow by blow about the night the big hotels burned fifty years ago. Fires are burned into your memory because they are so bright, hot, and scary. They stay imprinted on your soul.

There is a place in Hudson, New York, called the Fireman's Home. Retired firefighters live there. There is an interesting museum there, full of old hand-pulled and horse-drawn fire trucks. There is a collection of firefighting tools and they even have an old banner from Mahopac Falls hanging on the wall. There is a little cemetery there with the names of firefighters from all over the state. The retirees give visitors tours of the museum and talk about their fires. The first trip I took up there was with Jack Casey and Charlie Locke. I met a ninety-eight-year-old firefighter who told me about a fire in 1929. He talked about that one fire for almost an hour. The memory of that fire was still burning bright in his mind. It was a light he would never forget.

Going toward that light is often scary and always dangerous. Take, for example, a fire we once had. I had my pager on the open frequency so I could listen to the entire county. Our neighboring department, Putnam Valley, got a call for smoke in the area. Soon after, the dispatcher got other calls reporting the same thing. By the time the first member of the department got on the scene, he saw jet-black smoke billowing out of two windows on the second story of a house. It was around noon on an autumn week day so they knew they were going to be short of firefighters. They called the dispatcher and told him to send an engine and crew from Mahopac Falls to help. Being a work day, only three people showed up at the station: Walt Swarm, Tony Luccaro, and me. We jumped in the attack truck and raced over to the fire. I could hear by listening to the radio that Put Valley was undermanned and was struggling hard to keep up with the fire. As I adjusted my air bottle and strapped on my helmet, I pulled on the air horn that honked loudly over our siren so that cars would move out of the way. When we drove over the crest of the hill that overlooks the valley, we could see the plume of black smoke to guide us in.

When we arrived, the whole second story of the house was on fire. We pulled in just as the attack lines were going through the front door and twisting up the stairs. The Putnam Valley chief had a few people on the scene, but none of their junior officers were there when we arrived. Walt started pumping the truck and Tony and I volunteered to go inside. The chief asked us to go up on the roof and try to get in through a second story window. We climbed up the ladder to a low roof in front of an open window. I put my hand into the darkness and felt the heat. The fire and heat were too much for us to get into the window, so we climbed down the ladder and went in through the front door. Inside, the house was as dark as a tomb. I felt my way up the stairs, following the hose line. I could feel Tony hanging on the back of my coat to keep us together. The top of the house was dark and hot. We couldn't see anything. I crawled forward and bumped into the hose team in the upstairs hall. The Putnam Valley men and women were doing a great job putting out the fire so I just watched. There was a cord hanging down in the middle of the hallway. It was obviously a pull to a spring-loaded ladder that opened up to the attic. We pulled the cord, and then above us an orange and red display flashed over the ceiling. At this point the first attack crew was running out of air. Their low air alarms were going off so they backed out as a team. In firefighting, everything is done as a team. If one team member goes out, the whole team goes. This policy keeps one person from getting lost alone in a fire, one of our greatest fears. They passed me the nozzle and I began to climb up the creaking attic ladder. I opened the nozzle and let the water hit the fire as the black smoke and red fire mixed with hot gray steam. The water was pouring back down over me. In its short journey through the fire, the droplets became hot. I poked my head up into the attic and continued to spray as the flames rolled around. Normally we would have "vented," or cut a hole in the roof so that the fire would have someplace to go, but our forces were limited. After we knocked down the attic, I backed down the ladder where it was still pitch dark. If the fires in front of us and above us were out, where were all of the heat and smoke coming from? We had to search with our hands along the wall until I felt a doorknob. I put my hand on the door. It was hot but not scalding. I got on my radio and called the Put Valley chief.

"Chief, we got fire in a room on the south side of the building. I need you to vent the window on that side so we can push the fire!"

I heard the chief's calm voice echoing my command. "Echoing" is a big deal in the fire service. Oftentimes in the heat of battle we get excited and our communication becomes confused. Whenever a command is issued, the person receiving it "echoes" the command. So if someone says, "Pull two hundred feet of two and a half and the hotel packs," the person on the other end should repeat, "two hundred feet of two and half and hotel packs, copy." This is to make sure there was no miscommunication.

We waited in the black hallway, conserving our air. I did my best to slow down my breathing so I would still have enough air to finish the job. I was also beginning to get curious. Why was there fire in so many different rooms, each with the door closed. Usually there is only one source or seat of the fire. This fire, however, was burning all over the house in apparently unconnected locations. Something was not right. Suddenly my radio began to crackle. It was the Putnam Valley chief.

"Doc, the window is out and you can go ahead!"

I had Tony get on the other side of the door and then I opened it up. The room was ablaze; much of the smoke was sucked out of the hallway into the fresh air. The fire was now starting to breathe, so we had to hit it fast. We crawled in and saw the bed and the whole wall roaring and crackling. We pushed the fire and heat out the open window until steam clouded our vision.

Later, as the clean-up crews began salvage and overhaul, I walked through the building with one of the older and more experienced firefighters. He smiled as he looked around.

"Doc, do you notice anything strange about this house?"

"Well I noticed that fire was in every room with all of the doors closed."

"That's not all!" he said.

We walked into the kitchen and he opened the drawers. There was almost no silverware. He took me to the bedrooms where each closet had dozens of empty hangers. He showed me the master bedroom where there were no keepsakes, wedding pictures, or high school yearbooks.

"There are no valuables in this house at all. Everything that is personal or meant something had been taken out before we got here. Doc, this deserves a thorough investigation."

I was drinking a bottle of water when I walked back up to the hallway where Tony and I had spent so many intense minutes earlier. Tony was standing there with his helmet off and his face black with smoke. He smiled and pointed to the end of the hallway. Right ahead of us was a window. Just a few feet from where we were in all of that darkness, the light was shining; we just couldn't see it.

It reminded me of a story in Buddhism. A young rich man lost his memory wandering and living among the poor. One day he reached into his ragged pocket and found a gem. He had been rich all along and never knew it. The Zen idea is that everything we need is near at hand all of the time; we just need to be patient.

Many ancient texts talk about looking for the light. This can mean many different things, but it often meant the "path," or the "way out." Plato in the *Republic* tells of a search for light. This famous section of the work is called the "allegory of the cave." In this fable the people are chained to a bench in a dark cave. They have been there all of their lives and know no other reality. This semi-darkness is the only light they know. For them, it is reality. In this darkness, they see shadows that they mistake for reality. Then one day one of the prisoners gets free of his chains. When he leaves the cave, the light seems blinding at first. Eventually, he is able to look up and see the sun. He has seen the light. The allegory is about what we call "reality." Plato wanted to suggest that even though we all agree on what is real, we all could be wrong. He suggested there was something else, something brighter that was possible.

Religious people tell us that God is light. The soul has often been conceived of as light. The ancient (and modern) manuals on the art of dying, from the *Tibetan Book of the Dead* to Raymond Moody's popular *Life After Life*, tell us that the newly departed soul often looks for the light. In darkness we can be lost and cannot find our way back.

Philosophers are also interested in enlightenment. They make great efforts in thought to understand it. For many years I read and pondered about this idea. To be honest, I don't know what "enlightenment" is for everybody. I can only speak for myself. It has something to do with how we live every minute of every day. It does not take a Ph.D. in philosophy to be happy or to appreciate the preciousness of each minute we're alive. People complain that their lives lack meaning, warmth, love, or fulfillment. There is a choice we all make every morning when we open our eyes. We decide how meaningful we will make that day. It is we who decide if we will get lost in the darkness or not.

I got off from school early one day. I drove past the firehouse and saw a bunch of the men and women sitting on chairs enjoying the fall colors. I parked and went in. I got myself a cup of coffee and sat down and listened to the radio. Chad and Jeremy were singing *Summer Song.*

It occurred to me right there and then that life can be pretty simple. Maybe there are no secrets we need to learn. Maybe what is true is more obvious than we ever could have imagined. Perhaps that insight is the light that I had been looking for for so long. Sometimes after a long time in the dark we can step out into the light. That first step is the most difficult. But once we take it we will forever be changed. Sometimes it takes a long time to see that the light that we have been so desperately seeking has always been right in front of us.

20

Aging, or how to grow old without growing bitter

Age is a limit we impose upon ourselves. You know, each time you Westerners celebrate your birthday you build another fence around your minds.

Robert Riskin

Aging is not for faint of heart. In youth, we have an optimism and strength that can help us over the bumps in the road. As we grow older it is easy to lose that strength and that optimism. Once they are gone, the dark road ahead can seem scary indeed. One way to insulate yourself from this fear is to surround yourself with a loving community that can hold you up when you no longer have the strength to do it yourself. But what can we say about the nature of that community and how we can rely on it. Some of the great philosophers have asked this very question.

The English philosopher John Locke lived and wrote about a hundred years before the American Revolution. In Locke's time, a number of European thinkers were trying to understand what makes a community. Locke was especially interested in this idea because, just before he began to write, England had gone through a bloody and brutal civil war. He didn't want to see this happen again. To understand the fabric that holds society together, Locke developed one of his most well known ideas— the concept of the Social Contract. This concept had been discussed by a number of other writers. But Locke's take on it was fresh and interesting. The Social Contract expressed Locke's belief that for a society to work, there must be mutual agreement and civility among its members. He called the bond by which members of a society or community respect each other and preserve each other's rights the Social Contract.

Locke's ideas influenced the founders of our country, especially Thomas Jefferson. Our founding fathers took the idea of the Social Contract and used it to assert that a nation is a mutual agreement between its people and its leaders. To be legitimate, a nation needs the consent of its people. This has become the cornerstone of our democratic system of government. Community is the rock on which we all must stand.

At the Mahopac Falls Volunteer Fire Department, we also understand the importance of community. Before the firehouse is a business or even a team, it is a community. This is what volunteer fire departments have been in rural America for over three hundred years. They are places where food is cooked and coffee is shared. They are places where quilts have been made and birdhouses built. It is one of those community centers that can be the heart of any town. It is a place where the old and young alike can spend time together. This is especially true for those of our members who have begun to age.

Some people are comfortable with the passage of time. They accept the changes, and adapt some of their ideas about themselves and what they want. For others, growing old isn't so easy and can be very disheartening. Some people are so obsessed with being young that they can't face it when they aren't young any more.

It's difficult to grow old gracefully, but some people do it. We can learn much from them. We can learn how to grow old with poise and confidence. There are lessons that only time can teach though time is sometimes a harsh teacher.

"Hands on" experience is very important at my firehouse, as it is important at every firehouse in America. That's because fire is a tricky thing and each fire is a little different. It takes a great deal of experience to figure out how to handle a new one. As the old-timers say, "You can't get it out of a book." The lessons of firefighting are written in flames, and it takes a long time to learn how to read them.

Because experience is so invaluable, old-timers are a vital part of a firehouse. If anyone has any ideas about how he wants to change or improve things, he has to run them by the old-timers first. If they don't think the new idea is okay, that change won't be made for a while. That doesn't mean old-timers are against any and all change; nothing is farther from the truth. Some of our older members are the most progressive thinkers in the entire department. Some of our old ex-chiefs still keep up with current developments in the field. They spend much of their spare time reading fire magazines and talking to old-timers from other departments. They have seen enough to know that things aren't as simple as they sometimes seem to those of us who have just been in for a few years.

In the fire service, there's no substitute for experience. Old-timers made the same mistakes we make now, but they remember what they did wrong and try to prevent us from repeating the same mistakes. That's why at the Mahopac Falls Volunteer Fire Department, we don't cast our older members aside; we sit at their feet and listen to their wisdom. As Walt Swarm always says, "You should steal with your ears." He means we should listen to those who have experience and always take mental notes.

When I was young, I was too smart to listen to anybody. I did what young people do; I made my own mistakes. Since then, I've discovered an easier way. I listen to people who've made the trip before me and learn from them. I've discovered that I can learn from other people's experience without having to actually go through it myself. It took me a little while to catch on, but I began to listen to old-timers and respect the knowledge that they had gained. Wisdom may not be the same thing as age, but the two of them are related. From the old-timers at the Falls I've learned about fighting fires, but I've learned more about myself, about what's important in life and what's not.

We have many activities that honor the senior citizens at the Falls firehouse. One of my favorites is the "Old-Timers' Breakfast" for the "Sixty-Twenty Club." It takes time and work to get into the Sixty-Twenty Club: members must be at least sixty years of age and have at least twenty years of service in the fire department. Being in the fire department for one year is exhausting. About a quarter of the people that come in on a probationary basis don't make it through the first year or two. The pager goes off at all hours of the day and night. Fires somehow get going when it is pouring rain and the temperature is ten degrees below zero. Hose gets heavy, wet, and dirty after a fire. Racking it back on the truck is tiring. There are ambulance calls and rescues that can break one's heart and test one's nerve. So when I meet someone who has been in for decades, I give him the respect he deserves and listen to what he has to say.

The Old-Timers' Breakfast is an important and moving affair. Jack Casey and Camille Lapine work hard to prepare for it and we all pitch in to make it a memorable affair. Jack and Camille put in a good deal of time at the firehouse and end up doing all of those things that were supposed to get done but somehow just didn't. We usually have the Old Timer's Breakfast on a Sunday morning. I like to get down to the firehouse early to make sure the trucks are checked so we can get upstairs and enjoy ourselves.

The breakfast is held in the meeting hall and the firefighters do all of the cooking. The Ladies Auxiliary shows up and helps us make some decent coffee. We put some flowers out on the tables and even put on tablecloths—the mark of a really special occasion for us. Around ten o'clock the old-timers start coming in. Some of them have a tough time making it up the long stairway, so a few of us wait by the front door and escort them up the stairs or open the door on the handicapped entrance in the back. Seeing the elderly gentlemen with their canes and thick glasses, it is hard to imagine that they were once like us. Some of them are in nursing homes. Some of them can't make it over by themselves anymore. When this happens, the firefighters send cars and drivers and collect their senior members.

I remember a special visitor we had once, a small, frail old man named Harry Saunders. Harry was ninety-four, and had been one of the best firefighters that the Falls had ever had. The Falls was his family and he was loved. When Harry got too old to take care of himself, the firefighters worked to get him into the Fireman's Home in Hudson, the home for retired firefighters. It is filled with old men with many memories. If a department doesn't have anyone of their own up there at a given time, they often adopt a member to remember on the holidays. It's not easy getting admitted to the Fireman's Home. Because of their love for

Harry, members pulled a few strings to get him admitted there. Often they would go up and visit him.

Last summer, Jack Casey, Charlie Locke, and I went up to visit Harry and take a tour of the facilities. When we arrived Harry was not there to meet us. One of the retirees told us that Harry was feeling too poorly to receive visitors, so we didn't go up to his room. Harry died shortly afterwards. We had a moment of silence for him at the monthly meeting. Then we rang the bell that told us our brother had answered his last alarm. We will miss him at this year's Sixty-Twenty Breakfast.

One by one the old-timers come up the stairs to the meeting room. They wear jackets and ties, and their shoes are still shined. They are relics of a world that has gone by. They are men who did things with care and attention to details. Most of them didn't get rich or famous. They volunteered because it was needed and they answered fire calls whether or not it was convenient for them. They fought fires all night long and worked the next day without any sleep. They fought fires in driving rain and two feet of snow.

In their dangerous dance with fire, many of them were hurt and scarred. But there they are, walking a little unsteadily and sweetly smiling the smile of old age.

The smell of bacon and hot coffee fills the meeting hall. There is orange juice and all sorts of wonderful things to eat. Our old-timers load up on hot sausage, ham, pancakes, scrambled eggs, and cover the whole thing with hot maple syrup. These guys lived in a world that didn't worry about health issues like body fat and cholesterol levels. Usually at the Falls we eat buffet style; we all have to serve ourselves. But on this special day, we serve the old-timers at their tables. Often the radio is on softly. I remember coming into the hall and listening to the Del Vikings singing "Come go with me."

Over the last twenty years or so, we have become more careful about drinking alcohol at the firehouse. For the Old Timers' Breakfast, however, we make an exception. Almost none of the senior citizens drive, so we let them choose between two kinds of orange juice: Regular and "High Test." We put a "skull and cross-bones" on the high-test pitcher for those whose vision may not be as sharp as it once was. Some of the old-timers have a little high test, sit with each other, and tell stories about the old days.

One of the parts of the Old Timers' Breakfast that I like is the way the seating arrangements work. In many places I've been, the senior citizens sit on one side of the room and the younger people on the other. But somehow, we all seem to mix together well and share a morning.

Last spring the old-timers told stories about when the big hotels burned on Lake Mahopac. Some of the old hotels had nearly a hundred rooms. They were built out of wood and had huge porches with rocking chairs lined up in full view of the lake. The last one was torn down just last year. Then, somebody started to remember some of the old barn fires. Those were hot fires because the big barns were filled with hay and were old and dry. I heard some funny stories and some sad ones. I was listening to history. The old-timers are proud that they were firefighters and this history still lives in them. They wear lapel pins with the Maltese cross or the chief's trumpets. These lapel pins let you know that these elderly gentlemen were once firefighters or captains or chiefs. The world today is much different. We may have fancier equipment and we are more high tech, but we will never have more heart than these senior citizens had.

Last year, I helped one of the old-timers down the stairs on his way to the parking lot where a car was waiting for him. He was a tall man with a cane and thick glasses. I had met him only an hour before. He asked me if we could take a walk around the engine room before he left. He wanted to see the new attack pumpers. They are huge red monsters that carry 2,500 gallons of water and six firefighters with all of their equipment. They are fifteen feet high and thirty-four feet long.

He only stood in front of those modern marvels for a minute before asking, "Where's the Little Mack?" We walked to the other side of the station and there it was—the 1939 Little Mack. After the 1927 Stewart Buffalo, it was the department's second truck. It was the first brand new fire truck the department ever bought and we remain proud of it today. It no longer fights fires but it can still pump and perform. The old-timers make sure it's in fine running order. It's only about five feet tall and twenty feet long, but it's beautiful to us. It still has its original brass fittings. It still has some of the old coats and helmets complete with their battle scars and burns, hanging on it. The ladder is still the original wood kind, not one of its modern aluminum descendents. The old-timers like to talk about the old days in the firehouse as times when "the ladders were wood and the men were iron."

With great effort, the old gentleman got into the driver's seat. He held the old steering wheel with the word *Mack* on it, put his hand on the old leather seat and felt the dashboard. There's a silver bell and a crank siren. I clanged the bell and its sound resonated in the engine room. He was beaming and a tear came to his eye.

"You know, I used to drive this truck when I was a kid."

I didn't say anything. There was nothing to say. He kept sitting there and then seemed to apologize.

"I know it's not as big as the new ones, but this is a good truck. It has a good heart."

Yes, it has a good heart; fire trucks are like that. Each one has its own personality. If you spend enough time with one, you'll get to know it. I could tell that my friend had a good relationship with that truck.

He sat there a few more minutes before getting up. When we moved towards the door of the engine room, he turned and looked back at the Little Mack one last time. Then he headed off home to someplace far from Mahopac Falls. Maybe he lives in a room with his children or maybe he lives in a retirement home. But no matter where his home is, the Little Mack is still alive in his dreams.

There are two stations in the Falls. Our main station, Station One, is near the Red Mills Market off of Route 6N. We also have a sub-station, Station Two. It's near what used to be a farm called Houseman's Corners.

The sub-station is very different from the main station. It has only two trucks and most of the people up there are old-timers. On Sundays after the work is done, a firefighter from Station One can go over there and benefit by the conversation. I, for one, like to do this. We get our coffee and donuts and sit on the picnic bench out back if the weather is nice. The old-timers are often grumpy. They feel that the world has gotten sloppy. They complain about how we don't properly care for the trucks and the equipment. I always listen because I know there is a message to be heard here. This is the Buddha reminding us to pay attention to the present and see that things are done correctly.

The Ladies Auxiliary was formed in 1939, two years after the department was founded. I've been told that it was one of the first Ladies Auxiliaries in our part of New York State. The "ladies" do a great deal for us and some of them have been doing it for a long time.

We went to a wake and funeral a little while ago for one of the ladies who had been a member of the Auxiliary for fifty years. She was born in Mahopac almost ninety years ago. Her father had been one of the founding members of the Mahopac Falls Volunteer Fire Department and her husband, her brother, and her son were all members. It is rare to see such devotion in one family.

We went to the wake in uniform. Tony Luccaro gave a moving speech. He talked about the history of the Falls and all of the contributions that our sister had made over the years. When we were leaving the room, Walt Swarm told me that there was a lot of history in that room. We all said a prayer in front of the coffin and left.

I volunteered to be a pallbearer at the funeral. Tommy Stasiak and Tony Luccaro were there to help out. The funeral was in Saint John's Catholic Church, so some of our members who aren't Catholic were watching Tony to see when to stand up and when to sit down. After the funeral we proceeded to the cemetery. We carried our sister the last few yards. It was the least we could do for all that she had done for us. We had a luncheon at the fire department for the family and friends.

In some places people get old and they get lost. But in Mahopac Falls, we respect and honor our seniors. With the intense physical demands that it makes, fighting fire is a young person's game. However, the knowledge and wisdom of how to do it right must be a part of the equation. Mahopac Falls is a place where youth and age come together. Often on Saturday mornings, a group of us comes down and hangs around the coffee pot at Station One. Walt Swarm can be seen showing an eighteen-year-old how to rack hose or how to check a nozzle. I sometimes look at this and see an exchange of something more than firefighting skills. Walt is communicating a style of how to do things—a way to take care of one's equipment, a way to do one thing at a time and to pay attention to whatever one does.

John Locke lived through a difficult time. English history is filled with all sorts of conflicts—wars between different groups like the Saxons and the Normans, wars between the various houses trying to rule England, and religious wars between Catholics and Protestants. There have also been the wars between the English and the Scots and the Irish. Locke was trying to find that fabric beneath all of those differences. He wanted to discover the essence of what makes a community.

In Mahopac Falls I've discovered the essence of community, at least for me. One important criterion by which I judge a community is in how it respects its older people. The Falls is a place where aging can be done with the dignity it was meant to have. It is a place where I hope to grow old slowly, carefully, and with great love. Hopefully, one day a hot-shot eighteen-year-old will be rolling her eyes as a much older me tells her how we did things "way back when."

It is easy to see how some people get bitter when they get old. They lose their jobs, they lose their children, and they lose all of those things that made life meaningful for them. Some of the old-timers at the Falls firehouse don't feel this way. They got old without getting bitter. For they had a connection that they can hold onto even as the strength in their hands leaves them. What they put in to the place they more than got back. A community is what you make it. It is our choice.

21

Happiness, or how not to miss the simple things in life

Happiness is a Swedish sunset—it is there for all, but most of us look the other way and lose it.

Mark Twain

How can we be happy? This has been the one of the most asked questions in the great history of philosophy. Is happiness something so complicated that we have to read and study to realize it? Or is it so simple that the simpler a life you live the easier it is to achieve it? One of my friends at the firehouse, Jim McGinty, drives a propane truck for a living and drives a fire truck in spare time. On Sunday afternoons you can often find him with a can of Bud enjoying life. He never makes things more complicated than they need to be. I sometimes think to myself that he understands everything you need to know about happiness.

The Stoic philosophers had a great influence on the cultures of both Greece and Rome. Like us they wanted to answer the question: how can we be happy? They weren't very interested in life after death or the salvation of their souls. Instead, they wanted to know how to live every day so that they could be happy. One of the concepts they discovered was that to be happy we have only to look inside ourselves. They realized early on that a person could have wealth and still be unhappy. They saw people who had love and companionship and were unhappy. They noticed that people could have good health and still be miserable. If happiness is none of these things—wealth, love, companionship, health—what is it? They realized it isn't what someone had or whom someone is with. Happiness comes from the inside, not the outside. No fortune, no matter how great, can buy it. Happiness is being content with wherever you are. As the saying goes, "Happiness isn't having what you want but wanting what you have."

For me, happiness is a simple thing to understand. I've come to see that people have made the business of living more complicated than it needs to be. People spend a lot of time "searching" for happiness. But if we're searching for happiness, we're not happy; and if we're happy, then we're no longer searching. So the very notion of "the search for happiness" is a kind of contradiction. The more people search, the further away they get from their goal.

For people who give their time to the volunteer fire service, there isn't much time to be unhappy. There are always jobs to do down at the firehouse and we can always hang around in case there is a call. Some of my more intellectual friends talk about their lives in complicated ways. But for most firefighters, life never gets too complicated. They do their job and have a beer when the job is done. It is that simple.

Charlie Locke is a thin man in his nineties with a shock of thick white hair and a tan that he maintains in Mahopac Falls in the summer and in Florida for the rest of the year. He usually wears a brightly colored tank top, shorts, and sneakers. You might say he's constantly ready for action. He has a vigor and charm about him that could have made him a politician if he had had the desire for that kind of work. He's been married to the same woman, Eileen, for over sixty years. Charlie's retired now and every day he has the same routine. He arrives at the fire station main house and opens all of the doors around ten o'clock in the morning. He usually has some project going to keep himself occupied. But that's just an excuse for him to be there, putter around, and while away the time. He's really there to chat, keep an eye on things, and wait for a "hit," that moment when the siren goes off and the voice comes over the monitor that there's a fire or some medical emergency that needs the Falls to respond.

He greets everybody with his two fists extended and says, "Yo, men!" punctuating that with a little yell that sounds like a "Yewwwwwwww!" No matter what the weather or time of year, Charlie never loses his enthusiasm. He is there to give directions to lost truckers (who know enough to stop by fire stations when they get lost), information to anyone that wants it, and advice to those who have trouble throwing horseshoes or shooting pool.

Charlie comes from the Bronx and speaks with a pronounced Bronx accent. For a long time, he read meters for the Con Edison Power and Light Company in New York City. In July of 1949, Charlie left New York City and moved to Mahopac Falls. He had three young daughters and wanted to raise them in the country. He retired from Con Ed after thirty-seven years on the job. Charlie, however, was not one to put up his feet and go gently into that good night. He got a job at the county garage up the street from the fire station. The county allowed its employees to respond to fires during the day, so Charlie was able to drop his shovel or hoe and head down to the fire station when the old siren blew. He worked there with Walt Swarm for many years. He's seen hundreds of fires and has many a good tale to tell.

In the summer, the members drop by to hear Charlie's stories or jokes. He tells the same jokes over and over, but somehow they're always funny when he tells them. He usually prefaces his jokes with the caution; "stop me if you've heard this before," but the way he tells them is so funny that we never stop him.

A long time ago, the fire department wanted to make Charlie a lieutenant. But Charlie was smart enough to know that once he became a lieutenant he would have to enforce rules, argue with other people, and make enemies. That's not his style. Charlie understands that someone has to take responsibility for making things run smoothly, but he doesn't want to be that person. He doesn't confront people, gossip, or carry tales. If he tells a story about anyone, even if we all know who it is, Charlie will say "I never mention any names." He doesn't like to cause pain to people.

Although Charlie reads the paper every morning he doesn't bother too much about world events. He has more pressing fish to fry. Apart from his puttering around the firehouse, there are several other important elements of Charlie Locke's day. These include his car, his birdhouse and lunch. His routine rarely varies. His comings and goings are as regular as clockwork.

Charlie owns a four-year-old Chrysler station wagon that he maintains for hours every day. He is fond of saying "I'm very pa'ticlar about my car." and he means it. If there's a scratch, he wants to know where it came from. If it's not running exactly right, he wants to know the problem. If the steering or brakes feel unusual, he wants to take a look. He spends countless hours washing and cleaning his car. The care with which Charlie cleans his car is the same care he takes when pitching horseshoes or sand papering a piece of wood. He treats every task, no matter how trivial, as if the entire world depended on it.

He also builds birdhouses for some of the firefighters. These birdhouses are not just ordinary birdhouses. Heavens no! They have siding, gutters, balconies, window trim, chimneys, and look like somebody could live in them. When someone asks Charlie to build a birdhouse, he designs it to look like the home that the person lives in. Charlie cuts, nails, and talks as the time goes by. He spends his days building birdhouses, telling jokes and giving out wisdom for free.

Around twelve o'clock, Charlie sits down for lunch on a folding chair out in the sun in front of the open bay doors. By noon, if we're free that day, a good number of Falls firefighters are usually around. On a good day, when I drive up, four or five other members will be sitting there philosophizing. Art Brady and Charlie will usually get me involved in a game of horseshoes. I'm the world's worst horseshoe player, and I am lucky if I don't injure the spectators. The old-timers have tried to teach me how to turn a horseshoe over in the air as it floats toward the stake but I've never picked up the right technique. I grew up with the speed and sudden movement of basketball and the slow, deliberate world of horseshoes is one of those mysteries I can't seem to figure out. Charlie's eye is still as sharp as ever, and if he and Gary Link team up, they can lick all comers. Up at the horseshoe pit behind Station Two is a little bench. I sometimes sit on that bench in the shade and loosen my tie after my morning class. I watch Art and Charlie throw shoes. Sometimes Dougie Hyatt stops by. Dougie has a great laugh, especially when Charlie begins a joke or story with, "Stop me if ya heard this one…".

I remember one day sitting in the sun with Dougie, Art Brady, and Charlie watching the clouds float over the steeple of the old Baptist Church across the street. The oldies were on the radio.

The Diamonds were singing "Little Darling." We sat there and passed the afternoon with care and attention. It was a day worth remembering even though nothing happened.

Whenever people drive by, they beep their horns and wave to Charlie, as a kind of friendly tribute to him, and he waves back. He's a fixture in the Falls, a kind of anchor that helps keep the whole community stable. People appreciate him for that fact and honor him with a honk and a wave whenever they see him.

Around three o'clock every day, Charlie cleans up the workspace around his birdhouse project, puts his lunch bag back in his car, and sweeps the floor. He takes one last walk through the parking lot to make sure there are no nails or stones that might catch in the truck tires. Every year, in the first week of December, Charlie and his wife, Eileen, go to Florida for the winter. It's always sad to go down to the fire department after Charlie is gone and see how quiet it is. When Charlie was a boy in New York City, he lived across the street from a firehouse that had an old steam engine drawn by a team of white horses. He has seen the world change and he has grown old and happy as he changed with it while holding onto the things that are important.

A person is happy when they don't feel the need to be someplace other than where they already are. One of my favorite movies when I was young was *The Wizard of Oz*. Dorothy always wanted to be someplace other than where she was. When she was in Kansas, she wanted to be over the rainbow. When she got over the rainbow, she wanted to be back in Kansas. What she learned eventually is that she had always had the power to be happy where she was. She just never knew it.

This is what the Stoics talked about. Happiness isn't about being in Oz or Kansas. It is not about having a million dollars or going on the date of your dreams. It is not about living in a big house with a spectacular view. It's about what you carry in your heart. Two of the most famous Stoics had vastly different lives. One was an Emperor, the ruler of the Roman world. Another was, Epictetus, a slave who lived under a cruel and sadistic master. Yet these two people, with such different lives, both realized that happiness is an inner condition that involves finding comfort with one's own life, regardless of the external circumstances.

It was Aristotle who first noticed that, for most people, happiness is the one thing they lack at any given moment. A sick person thinks happiness is health. A poor person thinks happiness is wealth. For the lonely, happiness is company. But the Stoics understood these are only temporary fixes. If you really want to be happy, learn to live in the present wherever it is. Look right into the face of the here and now and bless wherever you are.

This summer the ritual of the firehouse will repeat itself as it has for many a year. You can often find Charlie and Art sitting in chairs in front of the open bay doors. The engines sit silently behind them. Charlie will be talking about how hot it's been or how little it has rained. Art sits there quietly and watches the clouds pass by the steeple of the Baptist church across the brook. They are sitting there waiting for a fire, or better yet, a game of horseshoes. You see, they are people who didn't need to go over the rainbow to find out where true happiness lies. Yes, Auntie Em, there's no place like home.

22

*Trust, or how to get burned
and still be able to reach out*

Trust thyself: every heart vibrates to that iron string.

Ralph Waldo Emerson.

We have already met the philosopher Friedrich Nietzsche in our conversation about "style." His works are meditations on what it takes to be excellent and to live an artistic life. He talked about living with character and strength. To him, hardships were good for us. Hardships, Nietzsche believed, teach us lessons that can't be gleaned in the classroom or libraries. He was seeking people who had what he called greatness, those souls who overcame extraordinary challenges. He wrote that a great person is some-one who, in the words of the Bible, has been "tested like gold in the furnace of affliction." Such a person is someone of character, someone we can trust.

Volunteer fire departments are not easy organizations to fit into. It's easy enough to join, but it takes quite a while to fit in. It took a long time for the firefighters at the Falls to warm up to me, and longer for them to trust me in an emergency situation. I never minded. Trust develops slowly over time and that's what makes it so precious. Someone once told me that if all of the pure gold in the world were put together, it wouldn't be enough to fill a single-family house. I don't know if that is true but its rarity is what makes it so special. Trust is like that.

A woman I went to graduate school with is now a psychologist in California. She is always talking about trust but doesn't trust almost anyone else. She runs therapy groups and does exercises with people who aren't very content with their lives. One of the exercises she does is supposed to build trust among the people in attendance. This is how the exercise works: you stand up in front of a group of people you've just met. You close your eyes and fall backward toward a concrete floor. The idea is not to catch yourself; you're supposed to trust some person you met fifteen minutes ago, who may be there with immense personal problems, to catch you and prevent you from cracking your head. This, my friend tells me, "builds trust."

When I was in California to give a talk, I visited my friend and watched one of these exercises in amazement. People were talking about "opening up and going with it." They were people who wanted to trust strangers they didn't know because somehow they thought that would make them better people. If I brought Walt Swarm, Tommy Stasiak, or some of the other firefighters to that group and let them watch those people for a few minutes, they would have one word for what they were seeing and you know what that is. The firefighter's vocabulary isn't always large, but it's vivid.

Trust is not something that can be built up in an hour, or a day, or even a week. Trust comes from experience and deep trust comes from years of experience. People who haven't figured that out can get hurt. There are good reasons why trust is hard to come by.

I remember when I first joined the department, I wasn't made really welcome. I'll never forget the first Friday night I came down to the bar. I sat there and watched the others talking among themselves the whole night. I butted into conversations a few times, but I didn't get very far. Charlie Locke was talking with Tommy Stasiak and Walt Swarm about some fire they had put out. I wasn't really part of that conversation. After several months, I still felt like an outsider. I thought about quitting a few times in the beginning. But I'm glad I didn't.

Now, after a dozen years, there are many people in the fire department I would trust with my life. I know that's true, because I've had to. Some of those firefighters are people who don't flinch when everything is in chaos. In the middle of the wildest call, Tommy Stasiak will be standing there calmly and Gary Link will be yelling at me at the top of his lungs not to get excited.

When I talk about trust, I think of an incident that happened a few summers ago. It was the bad car accident I described earlier where the teenage boy had wrapped a souped-up car around a tree and had to be extricated with the Jaws of Life. The crew that had showed up was Jack Casey, Tony Luccaro, and I. Even though he is an EMT, Jack is also a good driver and knows every little side road and trail in the district. If it's important to get some-place quickly, there's no one better behind the wheel. When we got to the scene, there were already other volunteers there. The car was smoking badly and I thought it might catch fire at any time. I crouched down and looked under the car. Gas was leaking out. It was going to be tricky extricating him. When there's gas and a possible fire, a rescuer has to be careful with power tools. I leaned in the window and took a closer look at the young man. He was badly hurt. I stood back and tried to decide what we should do next. Tony didn't need to do that. He knew exactly what he was going to do.

Tony climbed in through a broken window and asked me to hand him the medical bag. He put his hands behind the driver's neck and immobilized it. Whenever there's a traumatic injury to the body, we always assume possible spinal damage. We are never sure if the damage has actually happened but we act as it if it did. The spinal cord is as fragile as a piece of cooked spaghetti. Any movement can snap it and paralyze someone for life. The whole inside of the car was twisted and cramped. Tony was squirming around trying to get into a position where he could hold the victim's neck still. Finally, he did it. I started to reach in to help Tony, but my mind was on the gasoline and the smoke that continued to come from underneath the hood. I was handing Tony what he asked for, but my mind was racing. If that car exploded, Tony was in no position to get out. A few minutes later, the rescue truck arrived, Gary Link brought the jaws, and in a few minutes the door was off. A minute after that the young man was out of harm's way in the back of the ambulance. Tony didn't stop to be congratulated. He jumped in the back of the ambulance and yelled for us to start moving. As we rode to the hospital, Tony was totally focused on his patient. He didn't mention his heroics because to him his actions weren't heroic; they were simply what a rescuer does. From that moment on, I knew that I could trust Tony with my life. There was no question about it.

Around here, we fight fires with two things: water and trust. The water part is easy. We put the wet stuff on the red stuff. The trust part is more difficult. When firefighters get to a house on fire they have to go inside to really fight it. I've seen some departments that don't like to fight the fire inside the house. They stand safely back and spray water on a fire from the outside. You might ask, "What's wrong with that? If you put the same amount of water on a fire, won't it go out whether the water is delivered from the inside or the outside?" The answer is, "No, putting out a fire isn't that simple." When a firefighter sprays water on a fire from the outside, they are also pushing air at it. This can push the fire toward the opposite side of the house where the hose stream isn't as strong. To really get at a fire, a firefighter has to pull on his or her mask, take a deep breath, kick open the door, and crawl into the flaming belly of the beast.

The interior attack crew often gets set and waits until a hole is cut in the roof to let out the smoke and heat. If this is not done, and the front door is opened first, the fire might be sucked toward the door, which is a source of oxygen. If this happens, firefighters could be standing in the way of a backdraft, when a fireball rolls over the firefighters and can burn them badly. Many firefighters have been burned at one time or another. Stasiak got burned in the first two fires he was in. Walt Swarm got burned the night the whole town caught fire, forty years ago. A few weeks ago, one of the members on a hose line with me had both of his ears badly burned.

When the roof is vented, the front door is opened and the attack team goes in. Crawling low to keep out of the real heat, they advance into the darkness, looking for the dragon. This isn't a place to go in with just anybody! A firefighter has to be sure of who is in front of him and who is behind him. This is no place for uncertainty. There is no room for doubt. Trust is not a issue, it has to be assumed.

I've learned something profound in the fire department. Most people are afraid inside a fire, but some people will push forward.

Fear stops some people but not others. The secret is in figuring out who will stay with you in those moments of life and death.

Soon the firefighters are deep inside the fire. The only barrier between them and the fireball is a thin veil of water. If that water were to run out or slow down, they could be in serious trouble. They have to count on the pump operator to get the water inside and get it inside smoothly. The interior firefighters' safety depends on someone they can't even see. They advance blindly, trusting those outside to keep the water flowing and not let them down.

Among those who make the Falls a good department are the pump operators, the people who drive the fire trucks and operate the pumps that send the water through the hoses into the fire. Not only do they send water into the fire, they also have to unload water from other trucks called "tankers." Sometimes they have to siphon water out of a lake, pond, or swamp. When we have a big structure fire, one of the trucks is called a "source truck," and it goes to the nearest water or hydrant and taps into it. When the tankers have dumped their water into the attack truck, they return to the source truck and refill their tanks. In our department, the lieutenants are in charge of interior attack, the captains are in charge of the water supply, and the chiefs oversee the whole operation.

The pump operators can't make a mistake when there's an attack team inside. We once had a fire where four of us couldn't hold onto the hose because there was too much pressure in the line. The operator on that truck was a little rusty and we told him about it afterwards, politely but firmly.

A pump panel is a complicated device, with all sorts of gauges, dials, buttons, levers, and lights. A truck can have six hose lines running at any one time. A pump operator has to know how much water he's taking in, how much is going out, what the pressure is on both ends, and how his machine is holding up.

The oldest pump operator we have now is Walt Swarm, who grew up in the fire department and knows the trucks better than anybody. Walt was on the committees that "specked out" and bought many of the old trucks. Except when he was away during the Second World War, he's been at every big fire in the Falls in the last fifty years. Walt used to pump the Little Mack and was old and tough even then. I've been told that when there was a big fire, the Ladies Auxiliary would bring Walt a box of cigars down at the truck. Walt would pump and smoke, and when he had finished all of them, his brother, George, would chew the stubs until there was nothing left.

I remember being at a fire with Walt when I first joined the department. I didn't know much about pumping at that time and was amazed at how he did it. Even though Walt is a tough customer, he always has the time to talk about the fire department to anyone who wants to listen. I walked up to him while he was pumping the 1972 Mack. There were hose lines everywhere. Walt put his hand on the side of the truck and closed his eyes a little bit.

"Put your hand here." he said. I did. "What do you feel?" he asked.

"I don't know. What should I feel?"

He smiled. "The pump is bumping. There must be sand or something that made it past the strainer. We'll have to take a look at it later on." Walt smiled again. "When I'm gone, somebody's gonna have to know about these things!"

I smiled too. When Walt goes, there will be nobody who knows what he knows. It will take nature another forty years to give the Falls a pump operator like Walt Swarm. He has spent a lifetime learning how trucks purr and how a pump feels when a grain of sand is in the wrong place. He trusts his trucks because he knows every gear and nut. The firefighters inside a fire trust Walt to get them the water and Walt trusts the other trucks to keep him re-supplied.

A reporter at the *New York Times* was doing a story once about me being both a firefighter and philosopher. She stopped to talk to Walt. He said that he really didn't know that much about me. She then got back to me and told me Walt had said he didn't "know me too well" and didn't have too much to say about me. Now by that time, Walt and I had had a hundred adventures together. He had known me as a rookie, as an ambulance lieu-tenant, as an ambulance captain, and as a fire lieutenant. When I heard that Walt said he didn't know me very well, I understood. He has been in the Falls all of his life. He has known some of the guys in the department for forty years. Walt and I have known each other for only a few years. So that's my next goal, to get to know Walt a little better.

A few weeks after the reporter visited us, Walt and I stopped in the pub for a beer. We sat there a long time without talking. The radio was playing the Four Tops singing *Walk Away Rene.*

Suddenly after a long silence and sipping on his beer, Swarm suddenly spoke.

"You know pa'fessor, you're not so bad!"

I smiled. I knew what that secret code meant. I felt I had just won the lottery. We sat there a little while longer and the Chiffons came on. They were singing their 1960's hit *One Fine Day.* Walt and I sat and passed time and enjoyed the moment.

There are some experiences you can't get in any weekend therapy group. I don't trust people who talk about trust too much. I would prefer to look behind me and see Tony Luccaro or Tommy Stasiak when the chips are down. All I would need from them is a nod and I would walk into a furnace.

Doing something well, really well, takes a long time. The idea of "mastery" has always intrigued me. Pick something and stick to it. Go slow and listen to what the masters say. Be attentive to details and learn the nuances of any task you undertake. Listen with your whole body. The master is someone who has spent the time and passed the tests. The master is the one we trust.

Nietzsche knew that the superior person was one who had been tested. It is through these tests that trust is born and develops. At each step we have a chance to become more or less trusted by those who are with us. At a certain point the road becomes more difficult. It is then that those who want to lead have to go out alone and face the challenge. Ultimately, loneliness and hardship aren't bad things. They are also tests of character. Taking these journeys can make us better people. It is in these struggles that we learn whom we can trust and whom we cannot trust. In the fullness of time, trust blossoms. But you must be willing to wait. Trust is like a great wine. The great wines take a long time to mature. But if you have the patience, you will be rewarded. Unlike Walt Swarm on his way to a fire, it takes time.

23

The Journey's End, or how home is always closer than you think

Our Creator would never have made such lovely days and have given us the deep hearts to enjoy them unless we were meant to be immortal.

Nathaniel Hawthorne

Stories of secret treasures and hidden riches have captured people's imaginations for centuries. Stories are still told about the Holy Grail—the cup that Jesus drank from at the Last Supper. There are stories about a Fountain of Youth, somewhere here in the New World that gives eternal youth to those who drink from its waters. Alchemists and magicians in the Dark Ages sought what they called a "Philosopher's Stone" that would change lead into gold.

As a scholar, I have always enjoyed reading these tales and researching their origins. I find it interesting that people would believe that one cup, one drink, or one stone would solve their problems. I don't believe that. I believe that happiness, love, and courage come from inside us and grow slowly. No magic stone can gain them for us in an instant.

The modern version of the quest for the Grail is the lottery. I know people who think all of their problems will be solved if they win the lottery. I want to tell them that yes, some, or maybe even all, of their financial problems would be solved, but other problems would arise. No matter how rich a person is no one can escape from who they are.

I, myself, once set out in search of the Grail, the Fountain of Youth, and the Philosopher's Stone. The trail I followed, however, was a trail of words—marks in old books. In these ancient texts, I read the words of the great thinkers who had also wondered about why we are here, what we should do, and what we can hope for. Trying to understand the words of these ancient texts, I studied many languages and spent long hours pouring over old manuscripts in different universities. I spent years in museums and libraries reading the writings of great thinkers and writers like Plato, Homer, Descartes, and Hegel.

It took me nearly thirty years to see something very simple. I came to realize that reading a book or translating a manuscript were not the only paths to wisdom. Words are fixed forever once they are written down—frozen in time. But life is a constantly changing flow, different for each person at each moment. It is in that dance that we must look for what is real and what is meaningful. You can learn some ideas from words but there are experiences that can teach you things that books cannot.

Plato wrote dialogues about things like courage, truth, justice, and ethics. As interesting as it is to read his work and discuss it, it is not the same as being courageous, telling the truth when it might hurt, or doing the right thing even though it goes against one's own interests.

In my philosophy class at college we usually read the work of some great thinker who wondered about the questions that people still ask today. We ask about justice, truth, goodness, or love. We begin by asking what the author we read thought. Then I ask the students what they think about the subject. What does "love" or "truth" mean to them. No matter how they answer, I want to ask them another question to keep their minds working. This is called the Socratic method. If it starts to work, it can stir up all sorts of embers in the classroom. If it really works, we can start a fire. If the mood is right and the fire gets going, it will change the way the students look at the world forever.

A little while back in my honors philosophy class at Mercy College we had just such an exchange. It started innocently enough:

"Mr. Fiore," I asked, "What do you think 'love' is?"

He thought for a moment and said, "A feeling." A nice start, but I wasn't going to let him get off the hook so easily.

"Yes, but hate is also a 'feeling' so does that mean that love is the same as hate?"

Now he was starting to think. "No, it's a good feeling." That was a little better but we still weren't where I wanted them to be.

"Mr. Fiore, when I eat pizza I get a good feeling. By your definition, that's love."

Now he was getting exasperated. "It is a good feeling toward a living thing." Now we were getting somewhere.

"I like chipmunks; is this the same as or different from the love you feel toward your girlfriend?"

Mr. Fiore was now getting into a philosophical mood. "No, it's different, but it's hard to define something as vague as a feeling."

The conversation was now interesting enough for other students to want to give their opinions. A young lady named Audrey Russell had been waving her hand for a few minutes.

"Love isn't one thing; it's a lot of different things. You might love a pet, but that's different from loving your boyfriend or girlfriend. And then you could say that loving your boyfriend is different from loving your mother."

"But the question, Miss Russell, is not how many kinds of love there are, but what they have in common. We're looking for a definition that we can use to understand different kinds of love. Now we can start again. What is love?"

Soon the whole class was involved in the conversation. We talked about separating love from lust. We talked about friendship and asked if that was different from love. Soon the conversation took on a life of its own. The students were talking to each other and I had ceased to be an authority. I just sat back and watched. Now the students were doing the philosophizing; they were asking each other questions, and trying to understand what Plato was trying to tell us. I think if Socrates had walked through the door of our class that day, he would have felt right at home. The fire was really blazing. If I were lucky, it would be burning long after class had ended and I had gone my way. Every class is a common journey, with a beginning, middle, and an end. In a good class, we don't just find books. We find mirrors in which we can come to know ourselves better.

I think I realized my own journey had reached a certain plateau the night of the Mahopac Falls Volunteer Fire Department's installation dinner. We hold the installation dinner in October at a local restaurant. We were all in our dress uniforms and our families were there as well. It's strange to see the firefighters all dressed up, without their baseball caps and windbreakers.

Every year our fire department gives a "Firefighter of the Year" award. It's an award that many of our hundred members work hard to get. But that night, when the chief began to describe the winner, I realized that he was talking about me. That moment of that night, I knew I had made it. I had come home. I got up in my blue dress uniform and took the bronze plaque from the chief. He shook my hand with a warmth and love we had come to share through many adventures together.

I give speeches for a living in front of large and sometimes hostile audiences, but at this special moment and for one of the few times in my life, I was speechless. When the audience rose to give me an ovation, I was so choked up all I could do was to say "Thank you!" take my plaque and sit down. The chief thought I would say a little more.

"At a loss for words, Doctor?" he laughed.

Yes, I was at a loss for words. The installation dinner is the moment for our fire department to look back on the year as a family and reflect on our many adventures. As I walked back to my table, I shook hands with Tony Luccaro, Camille Lapine, and Tommy Stasiak. I looked toward the back of the room and saw Walt Swarm wink at me. They were still applauding when I got back to my table. Jack Casey, an intuitive guy, noticed I had a tear in my eye. He shook my hand and said, "Congratulations, I guess you made it, professor."

Yes, I had made it. It had taken years and it wasn't always easy. There were many times when I hesitated or had doubts about continuing with the fire department. There were conflicts and a hundred times I thought about quitting, I guess everybody does. But I realized at that moment that whatever sacrifices I'd made had been worth it. When the firefighters honor a member, it means something. They are not people who give praise easily and when they do, their praise means something very special.

A few minutes later, the lights went down, and the music starting playing. It was the Ricky Nelson's *Fools Rush In*. I thought that old Johnny Mercer song was appropriate for us that night because it talked about going places that angels fear to tread. That is where firefighters go, where angels fear to tread. That is where we rush to and hold our ground when everything around us is burning and falling apart. Inside that furnace we hold onto each other with trust and conviction and courage. It is an experience you will never forget, not ever.

I walked out on to the patio and looked up at the stars. Much had changed since I had first walked into the Falls Firehouse. Little by little I had stopped doing other things. I had stopped sitting Zen meditation. I had stopped writing scholarly articles. But most importantly, I had stopped being angry at life. In a sense, I had found another family, one that would accept me no matter what I did. I had found a family that I loved almost as dearly as I do my own son, Brandon and my daughter, Kelly. I had come home. Tony Luccaro and Tommy Stasiak were my new brothers and Walt Swarm was our loving father who cared for us by always encouraging us to be our best.

I think that I, like much of the rest of America, had gotten lost for a long time. Many of us have forgotten things that were once important—the traditional values that I've talked about in this book, like loyalty, trust, and care. We've looked instead for trendier, faster, more exciting things and lifestyles, but this search for novelty has left a gap in our trendy lives. Perhaps we are richer for questioning older ideas and values and for looking at things in new ways. I believe that part of us has to return to our roots. On that night at our annual installation dinner, I had found small-town America and its good heart. After years of travel, searching, and questioning, I had come home.

Yes, for me the journey is over. Like a leaf that floated in a thousand winds, I have come to rest firmly on the earth. I found peace in a little town in the Hudson River Valley. It was here I learned that by giving to others and joining in, each of us can find a sense of contentment that most people think is always someplace else.

Next Sunday, I'll go to the Mahopac Falls Volunteer Fire Department to check the equipment with Tommy Stasiak and Gary Link. Walt Swarm will be on his creeper working under the trucks. Charlie Locke will be sweeping the floor. When we're finished, we'll all sit outside in front of the trucks and talk about our week as we drink coffee from paper cups.

I have found those treasures that others have sought for centuries. That paper coffee cup is the Holy Grail, the water that shimmers in Lake Mahopac is the Fountain of Youth, and the boulder in my backyard is the Philosopher's Stone.

The brook flows by the firehouse, and the clouds roll past the steeple on the Baptist church. They move gracefully, without effort. We are like that brook and like those clouds. We need only to awaken our hearts to see the truth.

Afterword

This book has taken twelve years to complete. In that time, most things at the Falls Firehouse have stayed the same but a few have changed. Charlie Locke, who I loved so dearly, developed an aneurysm. In time it traveled to his great heart and we buried him on a hill over in Putnam Valley. Tony Luccaro had a heart attack and died one day after an ambulance call at just fifty-three years old. At that time he was still doing social work, coaching his son's little league soccer team, and was active in Special Olympics. His funeral and the events around it were among the saddest in the history of the Falls. Paul Fiori, the Mercy College freshman mentioned in chapter twenty-three, was killed in the World Trade Center bombing on September 11, 2001, an event that involved fire and EMS support from the Mahopac Falls Fire Department. The crooked steeple on the Baptist Church eventually was condemned and the whole church had to come down and be carted away. They rebuilt the church and steeple a little further south but the trees make it hard to see from the firehouse. Walt Swarm sold his house and moved into a smaller place on the edge of town. He now spends most of the year in Florida and he is not at the firehouse nearly as much as he was when I wrote most of the book. Art Brady was eighty when I wrote this book. When I last looked he was doing a Cha Cha at the Red Mills Pub at ninety-four.

In time, I grew in the fire service. After a few years at lieutenant I went on to captain. Eventually, I had the honor to serve as chief.

After I finish this last page I am taking a ride. It is a warm summer's night. The window is open and I can hear the crickets in the pond across the street. The smell of flowers is drifting in the air. I just got a call from Tommy Stasiak. He is sitting at home on his deck and invited me over for a cigar and a beer. The book is done and the lessons have been learned.

Life is short and precious. We should live every minute feeling like we have just won the lottery. I want to thank you for taking this journey with me. I hope you enjoyed the ride.

About the Author

"Dr. Frank" McCluskey took his Ph.D. in German Philosophy from the Graduate Faculty at the New School for Social Research where he won an award for the best dissertation in philosophy. After that he was a National Endowment for the Humanities Post-doctoral Fellow in French and German Existentialism at Yale University. He is a Full Professor of Philosophy and Religion at Mercy College in Dobbs Ferry, New York where he teaches both Philosophy and Leadership. He is currently serving as Dean of Mercy College's Online Campus. He has published articles and spoken at conferences all over the world.

Dr. Frank has had the opportunity to study with and dialogue with such thinkers as Hannah Arendt, Alan Bloom, Karl Otto Apel, B.F. Skinner, David Bohm and J. Krishnamurti. He has appeared on television with Joan Lunden and Dave Barry. For eight years Dr. Frank practiced Zen meditation in the New York City area.

Dr. Frank is an Ex-Chief of the Mahopac Falls Volunteer Fire Department. In his time there he has served as ambulance captain, training officer, and safety officer. Dr. Frank was honored as the Mahopac Falls Volunteer Fire Department Firefighter of Year in 1990. He is a member of the Fireman's Association of the State of New York, The Putnam County Chief's Association and the International Association of Fire Chiefs.

He can be reached at fmccluskey@mercy.edu

Appendix

THE REAL HEROES

To turn these adventures into a story that could be followed, a lot of details and people had to be omitted. There are over two hundred people whose names should be in the stories in this book. We did not include their names so as not to confuse the reader. A decision was made to take a few characters and follow them through these adventures. I would like to use these pages to acknowledge just a few of the people who are portrayed but not mentioned in this book. I apologize in advance for any omissions.

Mahopac Falls Volunteer Fire Department

Although he was away in the two years most of this book was written, Dave "Tiger" Beska has been at the heart of the Falls for a long time. Tiger is an Interior Firefighter and one of the best jaws men we have. During the rewrite, I included many adventures that he was the heart and soul of.

I would like to thank the chiefs I served under, including Tommy Kuck, Bruce Benjamin, Scott Harkins, Kevin T. Neary, Charley Castronovo, and Jimmy Degian. Their presence can be felt on every page of this book.

Many of the interior firefights portrayed in this book were handled by the Kilker brothers, Johnny Dearman, Bill Owsiany, John Topf, Mark Bailey, Kenny Robinson, Reno Regetti, Danny Sheridan,

Augie Dambrosio, Gerry Silcocks, Neal Bodde, Mike Miloslau, Jeff Boyle, Jimmy DeTomma, Haz Schweizer, Dave Lapadula, John Mulvany, Ron Link Jr. Tommy Haijak, Annie Link, Keith McCarthy, Chris Marion, Frank Andriola, Eric Murphy and Teddy Pollack.

EMTs who assisted in calls portrayed in this book include Gary and Phyllis Hoffman, Chaz Moore, Keith Puhekker, Pat Martin, Andrew Kristan, Jim Kempter, Liz Hughes, and Jim Petterson.

The jaws incident portrayed involved Randy Tompkins, Kevin Bagdon, Marty Kraus, Rob Mazzi, Pete Dandriano, Stan Zalesny, Chipper Arnold, Ernie Head, Terry Tompkins, and Don Kraus.

Truck drivers not mentioned include Al Detpatrillo, Skip Tompkins, Walt Prichert, John Scala, John Mulvaney, Jim McGinty, Connell Macken, H and H, Ray Forrest, Ronnie Link, Chipper Swarm, Scott Weber, Charley Liggio and Steve Larkin.

Exterior firefighters who assisted in these scenes include Bob Johnson, Ken Johnson, Greg Stuckart, and Bruce "Koopie" Koopman.

Artie Wisotsky, who was at the heart of all of the water and ice rescues over the past twenty years, is captain of the Dive Team and Ice Water Rescue Team.

Some of the senior members of the fire department include Ed Murphy, George Peters, Al Leblanc, Karl Neumeyer, Frank Deubler, Bill Heckett, Pat Perry, Andy Flately, Jack Upham and, Ernie Tsaldarus who guide us with their wisdom.

Mahopac Falls Volunteer Fire Department Ladies Auxiliary

Some of the ladies who worked so hard with us include Davey Beska, Barbara Bogholtz, Barbara Beska-Borowitz, Monica Butler, Lea Brennan, Pat Cunningham, Helen Dearman, Mary Delaney, Sheila DePaul, Doris, Carol Flately, Carol Kraus, Alice Kruz, Patti Link, Rita Manning, Carol Nesbitt, Joanne Netrosio, Joanne Russell, Gretta Upham, and Anita Williams.

Mahopac Volunteer Fire Department

Many of the things portrayed in this book required the help of our mutual-aid fire department, Mahopac. A few of those who assisted us in the stories included in this book include Chief Dale Smith, Chief Ed Scott, Tony Rendino, Joe Munch, Chief Jimmy Chulla, Jason Vicarrio, Jimmy Grunmann, Mike Revinson, Steve Starino, Dan Donnely, Jimmy Stasiak, John Goodrow, Kurt Beger, Dawn Stasiak, Chuckie Lewis, George Jones, and Tommy Beatty. A hundred other members from Mahopac will know the stories told in these pages.

Putnam Valley Fire Department and Ambulance Corps

The author wishes to thank Chief Ralph Neiss, Chief Glen Neiss, Chief Mike Pieller, Kristie Kroll, Chief Louie Longo, Joe Pie, Giles and Ann Spoonour, Helena Brown. Chickie Anderson, and Chief Ed McCarthy for their assistance in the events in this book. We would also like to thank Chief Mitzie Egans, Laura Egans, Mark Backus, Denis Orlando, Mike Konig, Charley Eberhart, and Billy Kirkwood for their friendship over the years.

Carmel Fire Department and Ambulance Corps

The scenes in Carmel should have included Chief Mike Hengel, Chief Peter Intrarie, Chief Bobby Effrom, Chief Tommy Keck, Chief Karen Tompkins, Charley Conklin, Karl Greenwood, Ambulance Captain Fran McCarthy, and firefighter Mike Johnson to name but a few.

Mohegan Lake Fire Department

Mohegan Lake helped a lot with the calls in these pages including Chief John Bonham, Chief Barry Brown, Chief Bill Hecker, Tim, George, Papa G., Freemont, and the excellent FAST team that is the pride of Westchester County.

Somers Fire Department

The Somers Fire Department has aided us during some of our dive calls and other events on our mutual border. Appearing in these pages should have been Chief Bobby Lutz, Chief Chubby Fallace, Chief "Cuban John", Chief Irwin Schroder, and Chief Scotty Rutkspin.

Other Friends

We wish to thank the Brewster, Patterson, North Highlands, Cold Spring, Continental Village, Putnam Lake, Yorktown, and Garrison Fire Departments as well as the Phillipstown, Carmel, Yorktown, and Putnam Valley Ambulance Corps who work in the area right around us.

Law Enforcement

Carmel Police, The Putnam County Sheriff's Department, and 40 Control Dispatching Center all figured into these stories. The police are the best friends the volunteer fire fighters have. All of the members of the Carmel Police Department will see themselves on these pages.

County and Town Governing Bodies

The Bureau of Fire and Emergency Services of Putnam County is our governing body and we could not get by without the help of such people as John Leather, Bob McMann, and Bob Cuomo. Our County and Town governments support us always, especially Bob Bondie who is both our County Executive and an EMT with the Mahopac Fire Department and Frank Del Campo, our Town Supervisor. Town Judge Jimmy Reitz is the son of a Mahopac Falls Chief. State Senator Vinnie Libel and Assemblyman Willis Stevens are often at our firehouse. George Pataki, Governor of New York State, is the son of a volunteer firefighter and a tireless supporter of our causes. Congresswomen Anita Lowey and Sue Kelly have supported us throughout the years. Without their support we would not function.

Big Moose Fire Department

We would like to thank the chief of Big Moose, John Vanderveer, a former member of Mahopac Falls Volunteer Fire Department, who was at most of the calls in these pages.

Mercy College

I wish to thank my staff at the Mercy College Virtual Campus, Hanny, Angel, Ralph, Boria, Karen, and Keva who have helped me live my double life.

Media

WHUD our local radio station is the music that accompanies this book and our lives at the Falls Fire Department. Eric Gross, a local reporter, the man who single handedly keeps our adventures in the public eye. The Journal News reporters also have always been on our side in the various issues of public safety.

0-595-22522-5

Printed in the United States
852200002B

9 780595 225224